Comical Fellows: Or The History And Mystery Of The Pantomime

Andrew Halliday

Comical Fellows;

OR,

THE HISTORY AND MYSTERY OF THE PANTOMIME:

WITH SOME CURIOSITIES AND DROLL ANECDOTES CONCERNING CLOWN AND PANTALOON, HARLEQUIN AND COLUMBINE.

Edited by

ANDREW HALLIDAY.

LONDON: J. H. THOMSON, 49 FLEET STREET, E.C.
1863.

CONTENTS.

B 2

COMICAL FELLOWS.

INTRODUCTION.

WISE men of all ages have affirmed that laughter is a good thing. It clears the lungs, shakes up the diaphragm, and loosens the fetters of the brain. How, then, shall we get a good hearty laugh? Shall we apply to the wit for his subtle refinements, and caustic jokes? They but make us smile. Shall we seek the broader drolleries of the humorist? They only tickle us. If we want a good roar, if we want to make our lungs crow like chanticleer, we must go and see a Christmas Pantomime. There is no fun like it after all. What verbal joke that ever was uttered can equal the exquisite comicality of popping a red-hot poker into the palm of the Pantaloon when he innocently and trustingly holds out the hand of fellowship to the Clown? Where is the witticism that can compete with sitting on a baby, and flattening it to the shape of a pancake? Even Materfamilias roars at that, though if anybody were to sit upon her baby she would faint and go into hysterics. Is there a more ludicrous object in the world than a policeman with his hat knocked over his eyes? Who laughs more heartily at that than the real policeman who keeps order in the gallery? Can you find us in the whole range of the drama a more telling situation than where the butterman slips down and hurts himself on the slide which the clown has made with his own pound of butter? Pantomime has the power of giving a comic aspect to everything. It makes even crime amusing, and yet without conveying a bad moral. The clown cuts off the head of a

dandy who is proud of his whiskers, and the children
clap their hands with delight. There is a moral, d'ye
see? He was inordinately vain of that figure-head of
his, and he was punished. Serve him right. The
clown is an arrant thief. He robs unwary tradespeople
right and left, and their discomfiture is the greatest fun
in the world. He is dreadfully cruel, and is for ever
burning pantaloon with red-hot pokers, slapping him in
the face, and shutting his head into boxes; but how we
enjoy it all! We will not stop to inquire why cruelty
is so exquisitely funny; but it is exquisitely funny;
nothing more so. And, burning with pokers, and jam-
ming fingers into doors, and stealing legs of mutton,
and squashing babies, are all such very good jokes, that
we can bear to see them repeated year after year without feeling weary of them, or voting them stale and
dull. Tell us a verbal joke that will bear such frequent
repetition. We think we could go on and prove that a
pantomime is the best of all dramatic entertainments.
Of what does a pantomime consist? Action. And is
not action the life and soul of every dramatic entertainment, from a tragedy downwards? There were some
ancient mimes who spoke so intelligibly with their
hands and arms that an intelligent spectator could
translate their story 'word for word' into language.
In those days (though it may have been very bad taste)
the pantomime was infinitely preferred to the tragedy.
And, by-the-way, it is said that the dramatic taste of
the present day is somewhat in the same condition. In
this little volume, however, it is not our intention to
deal in odious comparisons. We set out with the con-
viction that there are a great many worthy people, both
old and young, who love to see a good Christmas pantomime, and who are therefore sufficiently interested in
all that appertains to that favourite species of entertainment as to be desirous to have, within the boards of
one cheap little book, a succinct and readable account of
pantomimical performances from their first introduction

down to the present day. In following out this task, we purpose to glance, first, at the pantomime of the Romans; secondly, at the pantomime of the Italians in the middle ages; thirdly, at the pantomime on its introduction into England; and finally, to take the reader behind the scenes, and show him all the *penetralia* of the pantomime as we have it at the present day. We begin, then, with

CHAPTER I.

THE INVENTION OF THE PANTOMIME.

IT is very possible that pantomimic performances were practised at feasts or merry-makings among the Jews and ancient Egyptians, and we know that the early Greek drama largely partook of the nature of pantomime; but pantomime as a regularly organized theatrical entertainment was first introduced at Rome in the reign of Augustus. Indeed, that exalted personage is said to have been the inventor of it. It is certain, at any rate, that he patronized it most liberally, and that splendid pantomimes were produced in Rome during his reign. Mæcenas, Virgil, Horace, Ovid, and most of the literary men of the day, frequented the theatres to witness them; and in some of their works we have criticisms of the pieces and of the actors who performed in them. There were two great rival pantomimists at this time in Rome, Bathyllus and Pylades. The former was originally a slave in the household of Mæcenas; but his master was so delighted with the way in which he used to amuse his guests with mimicry and other antics at table that he gave him his liberty, and procured him an

engagement at the theatre. Bathyllus was a grotesque
and funny dog, who trode the lighter walks of pantomime ; but Pylades was of a serious turn, and excelled
in representing stories of a tragical kind. This Pylades
actually wrote a treatise on his art, in which he declared that no man could be a good pantomimist
(*chironomist* he was called, from the practice of
expressing himself chiefly by the motion of the hand)
who did not understand music, geometry, natural and
moral philosophy, rhetoric, painting, and sculpture.
' All which the poets have feigned,' wrote Pylades, the
clown, ' all which the mythologists have taught, all
which the historians have recorded, must ever be
present to his recollection.' The pantomimes in those
days generally represented the loves or exploits of the
gods and goddesses. The skill of the performers seems
to have been perfectly wonderful. The snarling old
cynic, Demetrius, after witnessing the pantomime of the
' Loves of Mars and Venus ' (in the time of Nero), said,
' I hear all that you are doing, for it is not only my
sight that you address, but your hands appear to
speak.' The people of Rome were quite mad at this
time about pantomimes and pantomimists. When Nero
requested Demetrius to name what gift he desired, the
old gentleman asked for a pantomimist, and assigned as
a reason that he had many neighbours of whose language his own people were ignorant, but that if he were
in possession of one of the performers in the pantomime
he need not provide himself with interpreters. The
Emperor Augustus was extremely partial to the pantomimists. By his command they were exempted from
that corporal punishment to which mimics and players

Fighting good

were exposed, and they were indulged moreover by a release from certain civil prohibitions. This, however, caused the fraternity to presume upon their privileges. Bathyllus and Pylades became jealous of each other, and their partizans got up rows in the streets, and this caused some of their privileges to be withdrawn. Shortly after this Bathyllus died, and Pylades had the field all to himself, which made him intolerably conceited and overbearing. On one occasion, when a critic hissed him, he stopped in the middle of his performance and pointed the man out to the indignation of the audience. For this he was banished; but the populace soon brought him back again. Another rival to Pylades now appeared in one Hylas, a pupil of the deceased Bathyllus. Pylades and Hylas contended together in the same theatre, and the passages of wit between them seem to have been exceedingly smart. In trying to represent the character of Agamemnon, in a particular line which termed him 'the great,' Hylas stood up on his tiptoes. 'That,' said Pylades, 'is being tall, not great.' The audience called upon him to do it better himself, and when he came to the line he threw himself into an attitude of meditation, thus giving an idea of the first characteristic of a great man. Augustus became alarmed at these disputes, possibly thinking them a little too political, and calculated to excite the populace; but Pylades argued with him, and pointed out the advantage which the emperor gained, as long as the attention of the Romans could be diverted by pantomimes from the consideration of their political subjection. 'Sire,' he said, 'you are ungrateful: the best thing that can happen to you is that they should busy themselves about *us.'* Pylades was evidently better versed in statecraft than the emperor. Hylas seems to have been a very irritating rival of the old favourite. But he paid the penalty of his provocations at last. A partizan of Pylades caught him one night, and gave him a sound horsewhipping on his own door-step. " 2.

In the reign of Tiberius the quarrels of the players grew yet worse. Blood was shed in the theatres, and not only were the lives of some spectators sacrificed in the squabble, but several of the emperor's guards were killed. It was consequently proposed in the senate to subject the pantomimists to corporal punishment; but it was eventually considered disrespectful to the memory of Augustus to repeal his act of exemptions. Regulations, however, were made for reducing the enormous sums which had hitherto been granted for producing pantomimes, and some provisions were made for diminishing the arrogance of the performers. Senators were forbidden to enter their houses. Roman knights were not allowed to follow in their suite, and their exhibitions were prohibited elsewhere than in the theatres. But in the course of a few years the disorders arising from these theatrical performances increased to such a pitch that all the actors were banished from Italy.

They crept back again, however, in the reign of Caligula, and soon acquired all their old licence. Nero found much amusement in their squabbles, and often took part in them. On one occasion, when stones and benches were flying about in the theatre, Nero actively participated in the fray, and broke the prætor's head with a footstool. The pantomimists under this reign were once more the *deliciæ* (the delights) of the

Romans. Again, however, they were banished; and
again they were brought back at the demand of the
Roman youth, who could not exist without their pantomimes. Under Domitian their performances became of
a very profligate character. The great performer of
these days, Paris, was accused of being too intimate
with some of the high-blooded dames of Rome. He
devised and acted a pantomime called the 'Amour
of Leda,' which won great applause, chiefly, it would
appear, because it was not very decent. The emperor's
wife, Domitia, fell in love with this handsome pantomimist, and was divorced in consequence.

The Roman pantomimists were employed at this
time not only upon the stage, but to amuse the guests
at great houses during dinner. They appeared as
carvers, and the flying knife which they brandished was
directed with a different movement to each dish. He
was considered to know little of his art who could not
vary his flourish as he operated upon a hare, or a hen,
or a lark.

There were amateur pantomimists in those days.
Stage-struck Roman youths paid large sums of money
to be allowed to play, and their friends seem to have
countenanced and supported them. Pliny tells a story
of two youthful Romans of equestrian rank who died
while exhibiting in the same pantomime. The scandals
which arose in consequence of these unseemly proceed-
ings led to the final suppression of the pantomimists by
Trajan.

The pantomimes of the Romans were called *Fabulæ
Atellanæ*, from Atella, the name of a town, where they
were first introduced on a small scale. The actors wore

masks and high-heeled shoes, furnished with brass or
iron heels, which jingled as they danced. Latterly the
fabulæ were designed to admit of a good deal of horse
play and knocking about, and it is not by any means
improbable that the actors may have been in the habit
of burning each other with red-hot pokers. It is very
certain that a kick in a certain place was held to be a
very good joke, and was always rapturously applauded.
The *Fabulæ Atellanæ* and the *Chironomists* are therefore
fairly entitled to be regarded as the first examples of
the pantomime and its modern performers—clown, pantaloon, harlequin, and columbine.

Before we come to the middle-age Italian period, where
we find the pantomime assuming more directly the
features which characterise it in the present day, it will
perhaps be interesting to take a peep into a theatre of
the ancient classic times, and see what sort of a place
it was. Every one knows that the first 'home of the
drama' was a cart, where the first actor, Thespis, stood
and declaimed his poetry to an audience of rustics, who
disposed themselves round him on the grass. Shortly
after this, Æschylus built a theatre of wood and constructed a regular stage. But in reading the Grecian
pieces—the comedies of Aristophanes for instance—we
must not associate our own stage with that of the Greek
theatre, or the light in which we shall view them will
be a very false one. The theatres of the Greeks were
quite open above, and their dramas were always acted
in the day, and beneath the canopy of heaven. When
a storm or a shower of rain came on, the play was of
course interrupted, and the spectators sought shelter in
a lofty colonnade which ran behind their seats; but

they were willing rather to put up with such occasional
inconveniences than to be stifled in a close and crowded
house. The theatres of the ancients were, in comparison
with ours, of colossal magnitude, partly for the sake of
containing the whole of the people, with the concourse
of strangers who flocked to the festivals, and partly to
correspond with the grandeur of the dramas represented
in them, which required to be seen at a distance. The
seats for the audience were formed of ascending steps,
which rose round the semicircle of the orchestra (our
pit), so that all could see without inconvenience. The
diminution of effect by distance was remedied by the
use of large masks, and it is said that the acoustic contrivances enabled every one to hear even at the greatest
distance from the stage. The lowest tier of the amphitheatre was raised considerably above the orchestra,
and opposite to it was the stage at an equal degree of
elevation. The stage consisted of a strip, which stretched
from one end of the building to the other, its breadth
being in very small proportion to its length. The
middle of it was the place where the performers spoke.
The front, towards the orchestra, was ornamented with
pillars, and small statues between them. The stage,
which was erected on a stone foundation, consisted of a
wooden platform resting on rafters. The scenic decorations were contrived so that the principal and nearest
object covered the background, and the prospects of
distance were given at the two sides—the very reverse
of the mode adopted by us. This arrangement had
certain rules. On the left was the town to which the
palace, temple, house, or whatever occupied the middle
belonged; on the right the open country, landscape, &c.

The side-scenes were composed of triangles, which turned on a pivot beneath when a change was required. The decoration was for the most part architectural, but occasionally, also, a painted landscape was introduced. In the back wall of the stage there was one main entrance, and at each side a door. As the middle scene was generally a palace, in which the great people resided, they naturally came on through the main entrance, while the servants and inferior persons came on at the side doors. Beneath the seats of the spectators a flight of stairs was constructed (called Charon's stairs), by which the infernal personages of the drama ascended into the orchestra and thence to the stage. The machinery for the descent of the gods through the air, or taking up persons from the earth, was placed aloft behind the walls of the two sides of the scene, and consequently removed from the sight of the spectators. Constant use was made of this machinery. In his 'Prometheus,' Æschylus, in the first theatre ever built, carried Oceanus through the air on a griffin. He also presented a whole choir of sea nymphs in a winged chariot. There were also traps in the stage for the actors to disappear through, and contrivances for imitating thunder and lightning, the fall and burning of houses, &c. In fact, in the very infancy of the stage, there was all the machinery for producing what is known in these days as 'Adelphi effects.'

The Roman theatres were very similar to the Greek, and exhibited few improvements. At first, by a decree of the senate, which was strangely opposed to all kinds of theatrical entertainments, no one was allowed to sit down in them. The audience stood all the time. The

first large theatre erected at Rome was built by M.
Æmilius Scaurus. It contained 80,000 persons, and
was adorned with great magnificence. We are very much
inclined to think, however, that some of the stories about
the Roman theatres of this time are not to be taken
without several grains of salt. For instance, Pliny tells
us of a huge theatre erected by Curio (in Cæsar's time),
which consisted of two parts suspended on hinges, and
formed either one or two theatres. 'In both they acted
stage plays in the day, and at night they wheeled them
both round and formed one grand amphitheatre.' They
must have had some very wonderful machinery in those
days. Fancy drawing Drury Lane and Covent Garden
together every evening! It is not a little curious that
at this time, when pantomime was all the rage at Rome,
rope-walking was also a favourite entertainment. A
performance similar to Blondin's was given in Pompey's
theatre in the presence of 700,000 people. The rope-
walkers were called *Funambuli*. It is certain, too, that
something like the trapeze was known at this period.
Juvenal tells us of *Petauristæ*, who darted their bodies
from a machine called the *petaurum*. The pay of
players at this time was from five to ten gold pieces,
but never more. Any reward that they received over
and above this consisted of crowns of laurel-leaves or
flowers.

In ancient Rome the pantomime died out with all
the arts and sciences, great and small—in fact, with
Rome itself and its civilization.

CHAPTER II.

THE revival of the drama took place in Italy in the time of Leo X., in the fifteenth century. The 'Sophonisba' of Prince Trissino was the first regular tragedy produced in Europe after the long interregnum of barbarism. The first comedy was 'Calandra,' written by Cardinal Bibiena. But the Italian taste, like the Roman, was decidedly in favour of the comic in its broadest and most practical form. Even their tragedies had comic scenes, as we learn from a description of the tragedy of 'Radamistus and Zenobia.' The piece begins with a combat of more than a hundred persons. The personages fight on the stage, besiege a place, and carry it by assault; and though the whole drift of the tragedy is intended to be as affecting as possible, Punchello is one of the warriors who frightens the combatants, parodies the best speeches, makes a jest of the hero, and behaves with all the ridiculous buffoonery of a puppet. Here we clearly have the first germ of the character of Harlequin. And in this same play, that the heroine might not want as striking a contrast as the hero, Zenobia's nurse is represented by a man with a black beard and a whig made of sheepskin, with the wool on. This tender female talks of virtue and delicacy, and is dreadfully frightened lest some one should offer violence to her charms. .

In process of time this comic portion of the tragedy was separated from the graver events of the story, and became a distinct piece of itself. At first the satire of Punchello was directed against persons and things indiscriminately, but in the new form of comedy the satire and fun arose out of the comic types afforded by the inhabitants of the various districts of Italy. The Venetians, the Neapolitans, and the Bolognese were all as distinct as English, Scotch, and Irish, and each one had a similar peculiarity. It was, then, to satirize and make fun of these local peculiarities that the characters of Italian comedy were invented. The original characters were Pantalone, a Venetian merchant; Dottore, a Bolognese physician; Spaviento, a Neapolitan braggadocio; Pullicinella, a wag of Apulia; Giangurgoto and Coviello, two clowns of Calabria; Gelsomino, a Roman beau; Beltramo, a Milanese simpleton; Brighella, a Ferrarese pimp, and Arlecchino, a blundering servant of Bergamo. The principal and most active character of this set was Arlecchino, or harlequin. The others were nearly all his butts, and he seems to have conducted his waggeries much in the manner [of the clown of the present day. He combined great stupidity and loutishness with much cunning and practical wit. This originally illustrated the character of the Bergamese, but in the subsequent development of his character Harlequin became universally entertaining without any reference to Bergamo. Addison, who saw a real Italian Arlecchino in his native land, describes him with characteristic magniloquence: 'Harlequin's part is made up of blunders and absurdities; he is to mistake one name for another, to forget his errands, to stumble over queans, and to run against every post that comes in his way.' It will be seen from this that the character of the original harlequin closely resembled that now assumed by clown and pantaloon. He had, in fact, the attributes of both combined. He was not a mere pirouetter and dancer, as he is at the present day; he was the principal character in the piece. This is attested by the nomenclature of pantomime. It was always 'Harlequin this,' or 'Harlequin that,' and this form is maintained to the present time, though harlequin no longer retains his old importance. The clown, in fact, now fills the place originally occupied by harlequin; and how this pantomimic transformation was effected will appear when we find pantomime transplanted to England.

Marmontel gives a minute description of Arlequino, as he appeared when transferred to the French stage: 'He is a mixture of ignorance, simplicity, wit, stupidity, and grace; he is a half-made-up man, a great child with gleams of reason and intelligence, and all his mistakes and blunders have something arch about them. The true mode of representing him is to give him suppleness, agility, the playfulness of the kitten with a certain coarseness of exterior which renders his actions more absurd; his part is that of a faithful valet—greedy, always in love, always in trouble, either on his master's account or his own, afflicted and consoled as easily as a child, and whose grief is as amusing as his joy.'

There is no prototype of our clown among the original characters of the Italian comedy. Giangurgoto and

Coviello did not fulfil the functions of clowns in our sense; they were merely minor characters, 'supers' in fact. Our pantaloon, however, seems to correspond with the *Pantalone* of Venice, and in the *Colombina* of the old comedy we have at least the name of the short-petticoated lady who dallies and pirouettes with our harlequin. Colombina, however, was originally a waiting-maid in the piece, and did not dance. The various characters spoke the dialect of the district to which they were supposed to belong, and all wore masks except *Colombina* and the two other waiting-maids, *Smeraldina* and *Spilletta*. At first the pieces—'Comedia dell' Arte' they were called — were trusted to the extempore wit of the performers, but subsequently plot and dialogue were written for them. It will thus be seen that these Italian farces were not, strictly speaking, 'Pantomimes.' The actors all spoke, but the fun was chiefly of a practical kind.

Harlequin became a very important personage on the French stage. He still maintained his Italian character, but he greatly extended the range of his satire. He did not confine himself to practical jokes at the expense of the other characters with whom he was engaged, but launched out into biting sarcasms at the follies of the day. He became the censor both of morals and politics. Harlequin and his companions were introduced between the scenes of dramas and comedies in the time of Molière exactly in the same way that we find them figuring in the early Italian tragedies. The most celebrated of the French harlequins was Carlo Bertinanzi, or Carlin as he was more familiarly called. His special excellence lay in the serious and stolid manner in which he would do something exceedingly grotesque and humorous. His gestures are said to have been almost as intelligible as speech, and when he spoke, a single word was enough to set the audience in a roar. Carlin indulged in a great deal of the practical fun which is now the principal feature of our pantomimes. 'When he slipped as he came on the stage, or, in a night scene, stumbled over a post or ran up against a wall, it was done with such a natural air that his audience could scarcely refrain from crying out to him to take care. The black mask, the little cocked hat, and the bat were then, as now, the insignia of the part. Notwithstanding the mask, Carlin's power of expressing himself was such that it was common to find yourself fixing your eye-glass on the black, senseless pasteboard and fancying you were watching an endless succession of comical expressions. As for the hat, he turned it to the most marvellous account as a means of denoting the various moods of his changeful spirit. When it was straight upon his head, with the edges turned up all round in the form of a diadem, it gave him an air of audacious defiance. A little on one side, with the corner drawn down towards the shoulder, it gave him a tender, graceful air, and signified that he was waiting for columbine, and that love was busy with his thoughts. If both corners hung like drooping ears on each side of his mask, he had encountered or was anticipating some misfortune, and the spectator might fancy tears rolling down his black cheeks; but if his spirit was elated with joy, both corners were cocked up with a swaggering, triumphant twirl that seemed to throw scorn in the teeth of fate.' Such is the testimony of Carlin's countryman, Fleury. English admirers of pantomime have spoken in similar terms of Joe Grimaldi; and, by-the-way, Carlin and Grimaldi were both of Italian origin. The Arlequin of French comedy eventually merged into the roguish and witty valet, who plays in the carpenter's scenes with the saucy waiting-maid. As Arlequin he exists no longer. In England he was reserved for, let us say, a better fate, for he still preserves some ghost of his identity at the present day.

CHAPTER III.

THE pantomime was first introduced into England by Mr. Rich, the manager of Covent Garden Theatre. The first entertainment of this kind was produced in 1717, at the theatre in Lincoln's Inn Fields, and was called 'Harlequin Sorcerer.' It was quite a novelty at the time and was thus described: 'A species of dramatic composition consisting of two parts, one serious and the other comic. By the help of gay scenes, fine habits, grand dances, appropriate music and other decorations, Mr. Rich exhibited a story from Ovid's "Metamorphoses" or some other fabulous work. Between the pauses, or acts, of this serious representation, he interwove a comic fable, consisting chiefly of the courtship of harlequin and columbine, with a variety of surprising adventures and tricks which were produced by the magic wand of harlequin; such as the sudden transformation of palaces and temples to huts and cottages; of men and women into wheelbarrows and joint-stools; of trees turned to houses; colonnades to beds of tulips, and mechanics' shops into serpents and ostriches.' The fertility of Rich's invention in devising entertainments was very extraordinary. Of all the pantomimes which he produced between 1717 and 1761 scarcely one was a

failure. It is not a little odd that pantomime should
have found its rise at the time when the public was
entertained with a larger share of theatrical talent than
had been known for many years. Garrick, Quin,
Mrs. Cibber, and Mrs. Pritchard were at Covent Garden ;
Barry, Mrs. Woffington, Mrs. Clive, and Macklin at
Drury Lane. Yet Rich had no sooner started pantomime at Covent Garden than Lacey followed his
example at Drury Lane. A few years after the production of 'Harlequin Sorcerer,' Thurmond the ballet-
master brought out 'Harlequin Dr. Faustus' at Drury
Lane. Rich regarded this as an encroachment on his
prerogative, and immediately produced 'Harlequin
Necromancer; or, Dr. Faustus.' This rivalry was
celebrated in the epilogue to 'Edwin':—

> ' Yon rival theatre, by success made great,
> Plotting destruction to our sinking state,
> Turn'd our own arms upon us, and woe be to us,
> They needs must raise the devil to undo us.
> Straight our enchanter gave our spirits wing
> And conjured all the town within this ring.'

Cibber thought it necessary to make an apology for
admitting pantomime to the boards of a great Temple
of the Drama. 'I would never have consented,' he
says, 'if there had not been a second theatre; but they
were obliged, at Drury Lane, either to comply with the
public taste or starve.' Pope had a fling at the pantomimists as a matter of course :—

> ' When lo ! to dark encounter in mid air
> New wizards rise—here Booth, and Cibber there ;
> Booth in his cloudy tabernacle sbrin'd,
> On grinning dragons Cibber mounts the wind.'

Cibber replied to this: 'If you figuratively mean that
I was an encourager of these fooleries you are mis-
taken, for it is not true : if you intend it literally that
I was dunce enough to mount a machine there is as
little truth in that too.' When a number of gentlemen in a coffee-house thanked Booth for the great
pleasure they had received the night before from his
performance of Varanes, and at the same time blamed
him for tacking to so fine a part the senseless stuff of
' Perseus and Andromeda,' Booth frankly said that he
thought a thin audience a much greater indignity to
the stage than the fooleries they had mentioned, and a
full one was most likely to keep up the spirit of the
actor, and consequently heighten the representation.
He also begged them to consider that there were more
spectators than men of taste and judgment, and if by
the artifice of a pantomime they could entice a greater
number to partake of a good play than could be drawn
without it, he could not see any great harm in it; that
as these pieces were performed after the play they were
no interruption to it, and for his part, he considered
profit as well as fame, and agreed, with Aaron Hill,
that it was not the business of managers to be wise to
empty benches.

Such was the attraction of pantomimes at this time
that the price to the boxes was always doubled when
they were played, and the receipts at the end of the
week instead of being 500l. were often 1,000l. When
it was objected that those who were desirous to see a
play were obliged to pay an advanced price for what
they did not want to see, the managers inserted in
their bills a notice to the following effect: 'The

advance money to be returned to those who choose to go out before the overture to the entertainment (or pantomine.)' This silenced the clamour, and the managers did not find their receipts much lessened.

The pantomime which Rich introduced was to a great extent a faithful copy of the Italian. Harlequin still preserved his proper place as the hero of the story. But Rich made one important alteration—he closed harlequin's mouth, and made him speak only in dumb show. Perhaps Mr. Rich had his own private reasons for this, and these reasons may be gathered from the following description of that celebrated person: 'His education had been grossly neglected, for though his understanding was good his language was coarse and ungrammatical. From an habitual inattention he had contracted a habit of calling every one *mister*. This appellation having been on several occasions repeatedly addressed to Foote, the latter grew warm, and asked him the reason he did not call him by his name. "Don't be angry," said Rich, "for I sometimes forget 'my own name.'" "I know," replied Foote, " that you can't write your own name, but I wonder you should forget it."'

Rich, however, though vulgar and uneducated, had a great deal of natural cleverness, and though *brusque* and insolent in his business connections, was a very estimable man in private life. He gave away a great deal of money in charity, and had many theatrical pensioners entirely depending upon him. As a manager he had but one rule in judging of a play, and one rule in estimating the qualities of his actors. If a play drew money, and showed a profit in the books at the end of the week, it was a good one; so Rich judged

the actor to be good who brought down the applause
of the house. It was the fashion in literary circles to
abuse Rich for having brought degradation upon the
drama by following such sordid principles; but better
men, or those who accounted themselves better men,
while they decried the policy of Rich, did precisely the
same thing. Mr. Garrick himself was not above
calling in the aid of pantomime, and it will be seen
by-and-by that the stately John Kemble was in despair
one night when Joe Grimaldi was taken ill and was
unable to play in 'Harlequin Hoax.'

As Mr. John Rich could not write his own name, we
may well believe that he did not write his own pantomimes; nor is it likely that he had much to do with
openings, seeing that they were for the most part taken
from Ovid and other classical authors of whose works
Rich could have known little or nothing. What Mr.
Rich did was to introduce pantomime to the English
stage, and invent what is called the comic business.
Mr. Rich was not only a very clever contriver of pantomimic scenes and tricks, but he was himself a very
admirable actor of harlequin. Mr. Davies, while eu-
logising Garrick, cannot help bestowing a word of
praise upon one who was the chief enemy of the high
class of art which Garrick professed. Speaking of
Rich, he says: 'Nor can we boast of any one man who
has, during the space of fifty years, approached to his
excellence; his gesticulation was so perfectly ex-
pressive of his meaning that every motion of his hand
or head, or any part of his body, was a kind of dumb
eloquence that was readily understood by the audience.
Mr. Garrick's action was not more perfectly adapted to

his characters than Mr. Rich's attitudes and movements to the varied employment of the wooden-sword magician. His leave-taking of columbine in one or two of his pantomines was at once graceful and affecting. His consummate skill in teaching others to express the language of the mind by action was evident from the great number of actors he produced to fill up the inferior parts of his mimic scenes. Pantaloon, pierrot the clown, and all the other various characters he formed himself, and to his instructions we owed Hippisley, Nivelon, La Guerre, Arthur and Lalanse—all excellent performers in these mummeries.'

We have seen that in Mr. Rich's pantomimes the harlequin was the principal character, the hero, in fact, of the story, and that he did not speak, but conveyed his meaning by dumb show; we have seen, also, that the clown was a very inferior part, less in importance than even pantaloon and pierrot. Oddly enough, the first innovation upon Rich's plan was introduced by no less a person than Mr. Garrick. In his 'Harlequin's Invasion' Mr. Garrick introduced a speaking harlequin, and in a prologue passed an eulogium upon Mr. Rich:—

'But why a speaking harlequin? 'Tis wrong,
The wits will say, to give the fool a tongue.
When Lun* appeared, with matchless art and whim
He gave the power of speech to every limb;
Tho' masked and mute, conveyed his quick intent,
And told in frolic gestures all he meant;
But now the motley coat, and sword of wood,
Require a tongue to make them understood.'

This was certainly a very high compliment. But possibly Garrick would not have been so ready to make

* The name adopted by Rich when he first appeared as harlequin at Lincoln's Inn Fields.

a public acknowledgment of Mr. Rich's excellence had
the pantomimist been alive to dispute the field with
him. Garrick had entered into rivalry with Rich on
his own ground, and almost invariably came off second
best. The rival spectacles produced at King George's
coronation afford an amusing illustration of this.
Garrick knew very well that Rich would spare no
expense in getting up his show. He knew, too, that
he had a rare taste in ordering, dressing, and setting
out these pompous processions; he therefore contented
himself with reviving the 'Coronation,' with the old
dresses which had been occasionally used from 1727 to
1761. This spectacle he repeated for nearly forty nights
successively, sometimes at the end of a play, and at
other times after a farce. The exhibition was the
meanest and most tawdry ever seen. The stage, indeed,
was opened into Drury Lane, and a new and unex-
pected sight surprised the audience, of a real bonfire
and the populace huzzaing and drinking. The stage
in the mean time, amidst the parading of dukes,
duchesses, archbishops, peeresses, heralds, &c., was
covered with a thick smoke from the fire, which served
to hide the tawdry dresses of the actors. During this,
the actors being exposed to suffocation from the
smoke and the raw air from the open street, were
seized with colds, rheumatism, and swelled faces. At
length the indignation of the audience could stand it no
longer. Tired with the repeated insult of a show which
had nothing to support it but gilt copper and old rags,
they fairly drove the actors off the stage by hooting
and hissing, to the great joy of the whole theatre.
Rich, on the other hand, fully satisfied the expectations
of the public. Such a profusion of fine clothes, of

velvet, of silk, satin, lace, feathers, jewels, &c., had never before been seen on any stage. The scenery, music, and other aids were all on a corresponding scale of grandeur, and the spectacle was shown to crowded and delighted audiences. Rich died while the spectacle was yet running.

The theory of the pantomime invented, or rather adapted, by Rich, was this :—Harlequin was the lover of Columbine, Pantaloon was her father, and the Clown was the blundering servant of Harlequin. The harlequinade represented the courtship of harlequin and columbine, whose course of true love was prevented from running smooth by the constant interference of her father, pantaloon. The pantomime generally opened with the abduction of columbine from pantaloon's house. Pantaloon would discover his loss and follow in pursuit, and when overtaken, harlequin used his magic bat to play tricks upon the old man and defeat his purpose. In this the clown was the assistant and servant of harlequin, and his function was to delude and beguile the pantaloon while harlequin was courting his daughter. In the course of their adventures, columbine was often rescued by her father and taken back home; but was always carried off again by her lover, with whom she is at last made happy with the old man's consent. The bat, or wooden sword, was supposed to have the power of changing copper into gold, cutting people in half, and enabling harlequin to jump through stone walls and vault over the tops of houses. The four colours of his dress had a special meaning. The yellow indicated jealousy; the blue, truth; the scarlet, love; and the black, invisibility; and they stood at the same time as the emblems of fire, air, earth, and water.

CHAPTER IV.

THE GRIMALDI ERA.

IT may almost be said that the mantle of Harlequin Rich fell upon the shoulders of David Garrick. It is true that Garrick never donned the spangles; but when Rich died he took pantomime under his special charge, and introduced to the public that great innovator, Signor Giuseppe Grimaldi, the father of the immortal Joe. It was Grimaldi the elder who paved the way for raising clown to the first place in the pantomime; and it was his son, Joe, who established the clown's claim to hold that place thenceforward. The merit of the innovation, however, was the father's, not the son's. Signor Giuseppe Grimaldi was originally a pantomime actor at the fairs in Italy and France at the time those fairs supplied the French theatres with some of their most famous dancers. He was first employed in England at the King's Theatre in the Haymarket, to act in ballets, and afterwards, in 1758-9, at Drury Lane and Covent Garden. At Drury Lane he was engaged by Garrick to play in a pantomime dance called the 'Millers.' He also played in a ballet called the 'Italian Gardener,' which was performed during the time that the dingy pageant of the 'Coronation' was running. A writer in the 'London Chronicle' thus spoke of him and the piece: 'Grimaldi is a man of great strength and agility; he, indeed, treads the air. If he has any fault, he is rather too comical. . . . Whoever composed the "Millers" has, I think, shown himself a man of genius. . . . I cannot, however, help observing that he has been indebted to Don Quixote; for when Signor Grimaldi comes in asleep on his ass, it is stolen from under him in the same manner that Gines de Passamont robs poor Sancho of his, and the same joy is testified by both parties in the recovery of the brute.'

When Grimaldi the elder first appeared in a 'regular pantomime' he played the part of harlequin. This was at Drury Lane, and the piece was called 'Fortunatus.' Clown, at this time, was an inferior part; but after a little time the Signor, at Sadler's Wells, adopted the part of clown, and combined with it the functions of harlequin. It was when he was playing clown at Sadler's Wells that he flung his son Joe into the pit. Little Joe, who was only about two years of age, was playing a monkey in the piece. In one of the scenes his father used to lead him on by a chain attached to his waist, and with this he would swing him round at arm's length with great velocity. One night the chain broke, and little Joe was hurled into the arms of an old gentleman in the pit who was sitting gazing at the performance with intense interest. This was certainly the first time that the clown was made the most prominent character in the pantomime. On several occasions at Sadler's Wells little Joe played a miniature clown, made up exactly like his father. An amusing anecdote of Joe's first appearance in this character is told in his 'Memoirs.' 'The Earl of Derby, who was at that time in the constant habit of frequenting the greenroom, to court Miss Farren, whom he afterwards married, walked in one evening and saw little Joe, in his clown's dress, crouching in a corner, where his father had placed him, with directions not to stir, on pain of a thrashing.

' " Halloa ! here, my boy; come here !" said the earl.

' Joe made a wonderful and astonishing face, but remained where he was.   The earl laughed heartily, and looked round for an explanation.

' " He dare not move," explained Miss Farren; " his father will beat him if he does."

' " Indeed !" said his lordship.   At which Joe, by way of confirmation, made another face, more extraordinary than his former one.

' " I think," said his lordship, laughing again, " the boy is not quite so much afraid of his father as you suppose.   Come here, sir !"

' With this, he held up half-a-crown, and the child, perfectly well knowing the value of money, darted from his corner, seized it with pantomimic suddenness, and was darting back again, when the earl caught him by the arm.

' " Here, Joe," said the earl, " take off your wig, and throw it in the fire, and here's another half-crown for you."

' No sooner said than done.   Off came the wig; into the fire it went: a roar of laughter arose; the child capered about with a half-crown in each hand.   The earl, alarmed for the consequences to the boy, busied himself to extricate the wig with the poker and tongs, and the father, in full dress for the shipwrecked

mariner (in "Robinson Crusoe"), rushed into the room
at the moment. It was lucky for little Joe that Lord
Derby promptly and humanely interfered on his behalf.
But, as it was, the matter could not be compromised
without his receiving a smart beating, which made him
cry very bitterly; and the tears running down his face,
which was painted "an inch thick," came to the complexion at last in parts, and made him look as much
like a little clown as like a little human being, to
neither of which characters he bore the slightest resem-
blance. He was called almost immediately afterwards;
and the father, being in a violent rage, had not noticed
the circumstance until the little object came on the
stage, when a general roar of laughter directed his
attention to his grotesque appearance. Becoming more
violent than before, he fell upon him at once, and beat
him severely, and the child roared vociferously. This
was all taken by the audience as a most capital joke.
Shouts of laughter and peals of applause shook the
house, and the newspapers next day declared that it
was perfectly wonderful to see a mere child perform so
naturally, and highly creditable to his father's talents as
a teacher.'

But though young Joe began thus early as clown,
some years elapsed before he had an opportunity of
raising the character to the importance which it now
enjoys. The new era of pantomime may be said to
have opened with the present century, when Joe
Grimaldi, in conjunction with Mr. James Byrne, the
ballet-master (father of the existing Oscar), produced
'Harlequin Amulet, or the Magic of Mona,' at Drury
Lane. This harlequinade was distinguished by several

D

unusual features, besides its success. Foremost among
them was an entire change in the character of harlequin and in the costume. Before that time it had been
customary to attire harlequin in a loose jacket and
trousers, and it had been considered indispensable that
he should be perpetually attitudinizing in five positions,
and doing nothing else but passing instantaneously from
one to the other, and never pausing without being in
one or the other. All these conventional notions were
abolished by Byrne, who this year made his first appearance as harlequin, and made harlequin a very
original character to the play-going public. His attitude and jumps were all new, and his dress was infinitely improved. The latter consisted of a white silk
shape, fitting without a wrinkle, and into which the
variegated silk patches were woven; the whole being
profusely covered with spangles, and presenting a very
sparkling appearance. The innovation was accepted
with great applause, and Grimaldi himself testified that
it was well deserved. 'For,' says he, 'Mr. James
Byrne was at that time the best harlequin on the boards,
and never has been excelled, even if equalled, since
that period.' This change, however, condemned harlequin to be a mere dancer and posturer. The clown
became the great mirth-maker of the piece, and Grimaldi's extraordinary talent gave it a patent to pre-
eminence for the future. In the opening of 'Harlequin
Amulet,' Grimaldi had to perform Punch, and afterwards to change to clown. His performance of Punch
was so excellent, that Sheridan tried to persuade him to
continue the character all through the piece; but
Punch's trappings were more than Grimaldi could bear

for a whole evening. They consisted of a large and
heavy hump on his chest, and another on his back, a
high sugar-loaf cap, a long-nosed mask and heavy
wooden shoes; the weight of the whole dress, and of the
humps, nose, and shoes being exceedingly great. Having
to exercise all his strength in this costume, and to
perform a vast quantity of 'comic business,' he was
compelled by fatigue, at the end of the sixth scene, to
assume the clown's dress, and so relieve himself from
the immense weight of the dress of Punch.

Grimaldi's clown's dress, however, was different from
that now in vogue. He made himself up to represent
a great lubberly loutish boy—a clown, in fact, as the
character ought to be. His trousers, large and baggy,
and well defined by the aid of stuffing in the posterior
quarter, were buttoned on to his jacket; and round his
neck he wore a schoolboy's frill. He did not chalk and
paint his face in the elaborate manner now adopted
(and which makes all our modern clowns look exactly
alike), but put on some patches of red, so as to give the
notion of a greedy boy who had smeared himself with
jam in robbing a cupboard. Grimaldi produced all his
effects by the humour of his acting—by the comic mugs
which he drew, by the grotesqueness of his pantomimic
action, by the *naïveté* of his blunders, and by the
genuine humour of all his practical jokes. He did not,
like the clowns of the present day, call in the aid of
acrobatism, and dance upon stilts, walk upon barrels,
or play the fiddle behind his back; nor did he seek to
gain the applause of his audience by astonishing leaps
and feats of strength. He trusted all to the force of
his natural humour; and such was his power, that he

D 2

made the success of pieces which were utterly wanting
in even the commonest accessories of a spectacle. The
famous pantomime of 'Mother Goose' owed its fame
and popularity entirely to Grimaldi. Nothing was
done for it by the management. It had neither
gorgeous processions, nor gaudy banners, nor splendid
scenery, nor showy dresses. There was not even a
spangle used in the piece, with the exception of those
which decked the harlequin's jacket, and even they
would have been dispensed with but for Grimaldi's
advice. The last scene was simply a pair of flats, and
there was no 'blaze of triumph' whatever. Yet, thanks
to the exquisite fooling of Grimaldi, 'Mother Goose
was an uproarious success. On its production on the
26th of December, 1806, it was received with the most
deafening shouts of applause, and was played for ninety-
two nights in succession—indeed, to the end of the
season. Grimaldi himself did not think very highly of
this pantomime. He always declared that his own part
was one of the worst he ever played, and that there was
not a trick or situation in the piece to which he had not
been well accustomed for years. Grimaldi was possibly
right about the piece, for afterwards, when another
clown played in it, it proved a very flat and dull affair
indeed.

It is worthy of remark, as a testimony to Grimaldi's
great genius and popularity, that a gorgeous pantomime
brought out at Drury Lane as a rival to 'Mother
Goose,' proved a complete failure, though it had all the
advantage of magnificent scenery and startling effects.
Montgomery played clown, but the business was so poor
that the audience began to hiss before it was half over,

and eventually grew so clamorous that it was deemed prudent to drop the curtain long before the intended conclusion of the piece. Grimaldi's great superiority over even the best pantomimists of his day receives a remarkable illustration in his contest with the famous Bradbury. On his return from a provincial engagement, Grimaldi found that Bradbury had been engaged at Sadler's Wells, and that he (Grimaldi) was not wanted. However, on the occasion of Bradbury's benefit, it was arranged that they should both play in the same pantomime, Bradbury sustaining the part of clown for the first three scenes, then Grimaldi taking it for the next three, and Bradbury coming in again to finish. Grimaldi did not like this arrangement. He was afraid that Bradbury had thrown him completely out of favour with the public, and that he would have no chance with him. The result proved otherwise. The moment he appeared Grimaldi was received with the most tremendous applause. Animated by this encouraging reception, he redoubled his exertions, and went through his three scenes amidst the loudest and most enthusiastic applause. This reception rather vexed and confused the other, who had to follow, and who, striving to outdo his predecessor, made such a complete failure that, although it was his own benefit, and he might reasonably be supposed to have a good many friends in the house, he was actually hissed, and ran off the stage in confusion. Grimaldi finished the pantomime for him; and the brilliant manner in which it went off sufficiently testified to him that all the fears and doubts which had previously haunted him were utterly groundless. Indeed, when the performance was over, Bradbury frankly admitted that he was the best clown he had ever seen, and that if he had been aware of his abilities he would not have suffered himself to be put in competition with him on any account whatever.

Like all great actors, Grimaldi threw himself heart and soul into his part, and felt all the emotions of it almost as keenly as though he had actually been the character which he assumed. The part of Orson, in the panto-mimic melodrama of 'Valentine and Orson,' was, in Grimaldi's opinion, the most arduous part he ever undertook. He played the part both in town and country on many occasions, but the effect produced upon him by the exertion of the last scene in the first act was always the same. As soon as the act-drop fell he would stagger off the stage into a small room behind the prompter's box, and, sinking into an arm-chair, give full vent to the emotions which he found it impossible to suppress. He would sob and cry aloud, and suffer so much from violent and agonizing spasms, that those about him, accustomed as they at length became to the distressing scene, were very often in doubt up to the very moment of his being 'called' whether he would be able to go upon the stage for the second act. He never failed, however. Extraordinary as his sufferings were, his fear of not being ready as the time for his call approached, and the exertions he made to conquer these painful feelings, invariably enabled him to rally at the necessary time.

Though 'only a clown,' Grimaldi became a very famous and important person. The highest nobility asked him to their houses, and even Lord Byron conde-scended to extend to him the hand of fellowship and treat him as a great artist. His importance professionally may be gathered from the fact that he was considered as indispensable to Covent Garden as the mighty Kemble himself. When he was suddenly taken ill, in 1823, the management of Covent Garden was thrown into 'a state of anguish.' The mighty John is said to have wrung his hands in despair. The public clamoured for Grimaldi, and nothing but Grimaldi would do. The managers at last hit upon the expedient of engaging Joe's son, who played for some time with a success which was chiefly owing to his being the son of his father. The 'fix' of the management was much talked of at the time, and gave rise to many epigrams and poetical effusions, of which the following is one :—

> ' The pantomime was all rehearsed
> And puff'd off in the bill,
> When full of grief, in Fawcett burst
> To Kemble, crying, " Hear the worst—
> Great Joe Grimaldi's ill."

> ' " Grimaldi ill !' the monarch cried,
> " Say what then shall we do ?
> Had I Macready at my side,
> Clown's part with him I would divide,
> And show folks something new.

> ' " But is it true, my Fawcett, say
> Has Fate thus spoke her will ?
> Is all we've done for many a day
> Cut up ? our hopes all cast away ?
> Is Joe Grimaldi ill ?

> ' " He is, he is,—that woeful brow
> Declares my piteous lot ;
> But come, cheer up, and tell me how
> To act in this dire moment now—
> For some one must be got."

' "I've heard," said Fawcett—as he spoke,
   Great Kemble felt less pain—
" He hath a son all full of joke.
Could he be got, 'twould take the spoke
   Out of our wheel again."

' Cried Kemble, "Bring him hither straight,
   Then puff him in the bill ;
The son will share the father's fate—
Be grinn'd at—I'm with joy elate,
   Though Joe Grimaldi's ill." '

But great as were Joe Grimaldi's merits, and great as
were his fame and popularity, he could not command
the high salary which a clown at one of the principal
houses obtains in these modern and ' degenerate' days.
Grimaldi made a good deal of money by benefits and
starring engagements in the provinces, but his salary in
London was never more than 14*l.* a week. For a very
long time after he had made his name it was only
about half that amount.

Those persons who are accustomed to think that no
good thing can come out of a theatre, or be connected
with it, will possibly be pleasantly edified to hear that
Joe Grimaldi, the clown, who was engaged during the
whole of his life in diverting the public with his quaint
tricks and antics, bore, in every respect, a most un-
impeachable character. In his manner, no less than in
his nature, he was a perfect gentleman. As a husband
and a father he was affectionate almost to a fault. As a
friend he was continually sacrificing himself for others.
In his conversation he was singularly pure and decorous,
and in his habits scrupulously temperate. He was never
seen the worse for liquor in his life, and in his last

days he consoled himself with the pleasing thought
that he could not recollect one single instance in
which he had intentionally wronged man, woman, or
child.

Mr. Dickens, in the ' Memoirs of Grimaldi,' which he
edited (and to which we are indebted for a portion of
our materials), makes the following remarks with regard
to the great pantomimist's style and manner: ' Any
attempted summary of Grimaldi's peculiarities in this
place would be an impertinence. There are many who
remember him, and they need not be told how rich his
humour was; to those who do not recollect him in his
great days it would be impossible to convey an adequate
idea of his extraordinary performances. There are no
standards to compare him with, or models to judge him
by; all his excellences were his own, and there are
none resembling him among the pantomimists of the
present day. . . . It is no disparagement to all or any
of these actors of pantomime to say that the genuine
droll, the grimacing, filching, irresistible clown left the
stage with Grimaldi, and though often heard of has
never been seen since.'

Old playgoers say that the only successors of Grimaldi,
who were at all worthy to be mentioned in the same
category, were Tom Matthews and Paul Herring. And
now, alas! of both these as clowns we must write
Fuerunt.

For the benefit of those young and rising clowns who
may have an ambition to revive the glories of the old
days, we print here Grimaldi's rhyming 'Adieu to the
Stage and Advice to his Son.' It contains the principles
upon which he 'acted:'—

' Adieu to "Mother Goose," adieu, adieu
   To spangles, tufted heads, and dancing limbs;
Adieu to pantomime, to all that drew
   O'er Christmas shoulders a rich robe of whims.
Never shall old Bologna—old, alack!
   Once he was young and diamonded all o'er—
Take his particular Joseph on his back,
   And dance the matchless fling beloved of yore.

' Ne'er shall I build the wondrous verdant man,
   Tall, turnip-headed, carrot-fingered, lean—
Ne'er shall I on the very newest plan
   Cabbage a body—old Joe Frankenstein,
Nor make a fire, nor eke compose a coach
   Of saucepans, trumpets, cheese, and such sweet fare ;
Sorrow hath ta'en my number—I encroach
   No more upon the chariot, but the chair.

' Gone is the stride, four steps across the stage,
   Gone is the light vault o'er a turnpike gate!
Sloth puts my legs into this tiresome cage,
   And stops me for a toll—I find too late!
How Ware would quiver his mad bow about
   His rosin'd tight ropes, when I flapped a dance !
How would I twitch the pantaloon's good gout
   And help his fall, and all his fears enhance !

' How children shrieked to see me eat! How I
   Stole the broad laugh from aged sober folk!
Boys picked their plums out of my Christmas pie,
   And people took my vices for a joke.
Be wise (that's foolish); troublesome (be rich)—
   And oh, J. G. to every fancy stoop!
Carry a ponderous pocket at thy breech
   And roll thine eyes as thou wouldst roll a hoop.

' Hand columbine about with nimble hand,
   Covet thy neighbour's riches as thy own,
Dance on the water, swim upon the land,
   Let thy legs prove themselves bone of my bone.

Cuff pantaloon, be sure—forget not this ;
　As thou beat'st him thou'rt poor, J. G. or funny !
And wear a deal of paint upon thy phiz,
　It doth boys good and draws in gallery money.
' Lastly, be jolly, be alive, be light,
　Twitch, flirt and caper, tumble, fall and throw ;
Grow up right ugly in thy father's sight,
　And be an " absolute Joseph " like old Joe.'

The great Joe Grimaldi made his last appearance at
Sadler's Wells on Friday, the 27th of June, 1828.
Dibdin's ' Harlequin Hoax' was revived for the occasion, and Grimaldi played clown in the last scene,
sitting in a chair, for he was too frail and decrepit to
stand.

The openings of the early pantomimes consisted of
little more than songs, choruses, and concerted pieces.
The dialogue was chiefly sung in operatic form, but
sometimes it was in prose. The rhymed ten-syllabic
verse is a comparatively modern introduction, and
punning is a more recent feature still. Many of the
pantomimes played in Grimaldi's early days had a
serious as well as a comic interest; indeed, they were
called ' serio-comic ' in the bills. Here is the opening
chorus of a pantomime (the ' Eclipse, or Harlequin in
China '), played in 1801 :—

' CHORUS OF CHINESE.
' Sound, sound the loo, begin your solemn rites ;
　Beat the big drum, transpierce the list'ning air !
　Dire apprehension every breast affrights ;
　The sun's vast eclipse, with dire portent, is near ;
　While, with acclamations, high heaven's power we sing,
　And look thro' nature boldly up to nature's King.' ·

A strange introduction to a pantomime truly !
All sorts of subjects were used for pantomimes at this

period, and the entertainment was not special to Christmas as in our day. Pantomimes were produced when-
ever the manager lacked an attraction, and were as
often brought out in June as in December. Who, in
these days, would dream of making the horrible crimes
of the French murderer, Dumollard, the subject of a
pantomime? Yet, at the beginning of the present
century, an exactly similar story—that of the 'Golden
Farmer'—was used for that purpose. The 'Golden
Farmer,' so called from always paying in gold, was
famous for his plundering exploits in almost every
county in England; and yet he ostensibly followed the
business of a farmer. It was his custom, as soon as he
paid any creditor, to disguise himself, waylay, and not
only oblige him to return the money he had received,
but add whatever else he was in possession of. These
exploits are the subject of the pantomime, thus : A rich
Berkshire grazier, having waited on the farmer for his
rent, was received with the greatest friendship, and he
and his daughter, her lover, and servant, entertained
with all the rustic cheer and merriment the farmer's
home afforded. His servants amused them with dancing,
and in return his ploughboy was honoured with the
hand of the grazier's daughter as his partner in the
dance: a mutual passion took place, which there appeared little prospect of their ever being able to gratify,
the lady being betrothed, and at the same time viewed
with eyes of affection by the Golden Farmer. The
farmer, seeing the ploughboy's glances, determines not
long to suffer his rivalry ; and, on the grazier and his
daughter taking leave, resolves, with the aid of his
graceless servant, Long Robin, to follow and plunder
them, and at the same time to seize the daughter, com-

pelling the ploughboy to be an accomplice, in order to
betray him into the hands of justice. Accordingly,
they overtake his recent visitors, and are about to rob
them, when the ploughboy assumes the character of
harlequin, and escapes with the object of his affection,
who becomes columbine.

The following are some specimens of the operatic
dialogue :—

> FARMER. Gladly money I lend, where I honesty find.
> COTTAGERS. To the poor he's a friend.
> RUSTICS. To his servants he's kind.
> ALL. And the milk of humanity never flowed warmer
> Than in the rich veins of the Golden Farmer.

The grazier and his daughter take leave, and set out
on their journey homeward :—

> FARMER (to Grazier). Farewell! may your steeds speed ye quick
> o'er the plain !
> (aside) Though, if my nag's sound, they'll soon be overta'en.
> (To Colum.) May you rest on life's journey, secure from alarms !
> (aside) Nor dream of my love, till you're clasped in my arms.
> (To Clown) May no robbers alarm you till I view your fright !
> To our next merry meeting. Good evening.
> ALL. Good night.

And then, in the hour of danger, a guardian Nymph
interposes, like the good fairy, with—

> ' Then, swift as thought, like Fancy's queen,
> For safety thus I change the scene ;
> And warn ye dread in evil hour,
> Alike the Farmer's and the robber's power.'

The literary portion of the pantomime of the 'good
school ' is poor stuff in comparison with the witty and
polished introductions furnished in these days by Mr.
E. L. Blanchard, Mr. Henry Byron, and others.

CHAPTER V.

PANTOMIME OF THE PRESENT.

PLAYGOERS of the old school would describe the period
upon which we are now entering as marking the 'decline and fall of pantomime.' In Grimaldi's days the
pantomime depended for its success upon the pantomimic powers of those who performed in it. It was the
exquisite fooling of clown, pantaloon, harlequin, and
columbine that drew crowded audiences and brought
down the applause. But in the period that succeeded,
when there were no worthy successors of Grimaldi and
Bologna (the harlequin), it was found necessary to call
in the aid of gorgeous dresses, magnificent scenery, and
the most elaborate mechanical effects. We have seen
that Joe Grimaldi could get on without these aids, and
that his grimacing and filching, and kicking and slapping, were so comical in themselves that the public
desired nothing else. True pantomime may therefore
be said to have declined when there were no longer
representatives of the various characters who could hold
the attention of the public by their own unaided talents.
The same thing, indeed, may be said of the drama generally; and it would really appear that the race of great
pantomimists and great tragedians died out together.

Scenery, dresses, and effects were called into the aid
of the tragedians and the pantomimists about the same

time. The great innovator of this period was Mr.
Planché. In the year 1822, this gentleman represented
to Mr. Charles Kemble that there was something (to
him) very absurd in seeing twelve or twenty-four
soldiers, in red tunics trimmed with lace, and as many
in blue similarly ornamented, representing the armies
of England and France, in 'King John' in one night,
and in 'Henry V.' the next; or fighting, in the reign
of Henry IV., by 'Shrewsbury clock' at . Bosworth
Field under Richard on the Monday following. Mr. C.
Kemble, who was then contemplating the revival of
Shakespere's historical plays, had the courage (as a
manager) to agree with Mr. Planché, and that gentleman
was engaged to 'reform' the dress and property plan
'altogether.' Under his direction King John appeared
in his habit as he lived, surrounded by his mantled
courtiers and mail-clad knights, and the public, at the
first sight of this reformation, expressed the most
rapturous delight, though many of the old actors,
including Farley and Fawcett, could never get over
their early impressions. Mr. Planché tells us that
Liston thought to the last that Prometheus, instead of
a Phrygian cap, tunic, and trousers, should have been
dressed like a great lubberly boy in a red jacket and
nankeens, with a pinafore all besmeared with lollipop.
It will readily be seen that the adoption of elegant costumes necessitated the painting of appropriate scenery.
A pair of dingy 'flats' harmonized very well with a
Prometheus in a jacket and trousers ; but the Phrygian
cap and the elegant tunic required something better.
Consequently elegant and appropriate scenery followed
upon elegant and correct costumes. The immediate

effect of this innovation was to stimulate the pantomimists to efforts such as had never been required before. When Farley saw Kemble getting up 'King John,' 'regardless of expense,' and on a 'scale of magnificence never before attempted,' he piteously exclaimed, 'If Shakespere is to be produced with such splendour and attention to costume, what am I to do for the holidays?' Of course when the holidays came it was necessary, if possible, to surpass even the splendour of 'King John,' and the efforts made in this direction led eventually to the introduction of what is known in these days as transformation-scenes. Originally the transformation was simply the changing of the characters in the opening into clown, pantaloon, harlequin, and columbine; but now, when the characters changed, the scene changed also, and the effect of the whole picture was heightened by tinsel and coloured fires. For a good many years, however, the transformation-scene was nothing better than a pair of flats, representing the Realms of Bliss in painted perspective. The days of elaborate magnificence, of descending clouds, and opening bowers, of floating fairies and trickling waterfalls, of moving pieces, and gradually-unfolding pictures, were yet to come. And they came when Mr. William Beverley began to paint the scenes for Mr. Planché's elegant extravaganzas somewhere about the year 1847. Mr. Beverley reached the *ne plus ultra* of his new style of scenic art almost in his very first examples. There is scarcely anything that we have seen since which has eclipsed the beauty and magnificence of the scenery of the 'Golden Branch,' the 'King of the Peacocks,' and the 'Island of Jewels,' 'But, alas!' exclaims Mr.

Planché, '"this effect defective came by the cause."
Year after year Mr. Beverley's powers were taxed to
outdo his former outdoings. The *last* scene became the
first in the estimation of the management. The most
complicated machinery, the most costly materials, were
annually put into requisition, until their bacon, was so
buttered that it was impossible to save it. As to me, I
was positively painted out. Nothing was considered
brilliant but the last scene. Dutch metal was in the
ascendant. It was no longer even painting, but up-
holstery.' Madame Vestris paid between 60*l.* and 70*l.*
for the gold tissue for the dresses of the supernumeraries
alone in the last scene of 'Once upon a Time.'

Pantomime had now to contend with two rivals—with
the historical splendours of tragedy and the fairy magnificence of burlesque. In the effort to outdo both,
two transformation-scenes were introduced, one at the
end of the opening and another at the end of the comic
business. For a little time pantomime seemed in
danger of being entirely superseded by extravaganza,
and in order to save itself it went into partnership with
the new form of entertainment; and for a while we had
extravaganza for the opening and pantomime for the
finish, without any attempt at connecting the two
stories, or the two sets of characters. On two occasions,
not long ago, the authors, feeling their dignity hurt by
having 'comic scenes' tacked on to their burlesque
poetry, insisted that the curtain should fall between the
parts. But this was when pantomime had survived its
danger, and was beginning to be considered a necessary
adjunct to burlesque. During the period that pantomime was seriously assailed by extravaganza, it had to

E

resort to many shifts besides that of offering the public
two transformations. The clowns, distrusting those
modes of operation which proved so effective in Grimaldi's hands (and feet), became acrobats and posturers.
They endeavoured to recommend themselves to the
public by dancing on stilts, by walking on barrels, by
playing the fiddle with their knees, and by various other
devices of the kind, which had really nothing to do with
the business of the scene. In fact, they sought to
make up for want of humour by their agility. And
straining their efforts still further, they treated the
public to two sets of performers in the same pantomime
—two clowns and two pantaloons, &c.—each set playing
in alternate scenes, 'as if,' as a critic observed, 'by
doubling the dose of dulness they were presenting the
public with double their money's worth.' But there is
nothing easier than to be sarcastic and uncharitable at
the same time. It is possibly a very fair subject of
complaint that the pantomime in our days has lost the
meaning and unity of purpose which it had originally;
but certainly those persons must be hard to please who
cannot find real enjoyment in the pantomimes which
are annually produced at Drury Lane, Covent Garden,
and the Princess's. We would particularly specify the
pantomimes which have recently been produced at the
last-mentioned house. 'Jack the Giant Killer,' 'Robinson Crusoe,' and 'Whittington and his Cat,' contained
all the true elements of the genuine Christmas pantomime. The openings were short and strictly pantomimic; the characters, with the exception of the ladies,
appeared in grotesque masks, and accompanied their
rhyming dialogue with an abundance of pantomimic

gesture; there was a well-defined connection between the characters in the opening and the mimes who followed them; and the 'comic business,' especially in 'Whittington,' depended for its success in a great degree upon the humorous acting of the clown. We never saw Grimaldi; but from what we have heard and read of that celebrated mime we should say that Mr. Hildyard, who played clown at the Princess's in 'Whittington and his Cat' during the season of 1861–2, is no unworthy disciple of his school. He appeared to us to be the perfection of a grinning, filching, blundering, mischief-making clown. Grimaldi might have been better, but if we can boast clowns like Mr. Hildyard and Mr. Boleno, pantaloons like Mr. Paulo and Mr. Barnes, and such pantomimists as the Paynes and the Leclercqs for the openings, we cannot see that there is any just ground for asserting that the pantomimic art has suffered serious decline.

CHAPTER VI.

THE READING OF THE PANTOMIME.

ABOUT six or eight weeks before Boxing-night, the author, the stage-manager, and the prompter meet what may be called the pantomimic staff, and general suggestions are made, objected to, altered and received. The staff consists of:—

Mr. Size, the scene-painter.
Boggles, the master-carpenter.
Lotus and Miss Crooner, the costumiers;
and Slocum, the property-man.

Mr. Ernest Hammer, the stage-manager, and Mr. Syllabus, the author, are in conference with Mr. H. B. Writhe, the eminent pantomimist, who plays the principal part in the opening, and Mr. Pablo Johnson, Herr Bellonetti, and Mr. Alf. Scithers, the clown, harlequin and pantaloon. Neither Mdlle. Celestine, the columbine, nor Signor Van Diemen Contorti, the sprite, is present; Mdlle. being engaged as première danseuse in the provinces, and the Signor nightly perilling his life at the Great Transatlantic International Circus.

Mr. Size is a tall, thin, pale-faced gentleman in spectacles, with a cracked voice and a very subdued manner. He is attired in a splashed canvas jacket and trousers, and has the air of an experimental chemist disguised as a stonemason.

Mr. Boggles, the master-carpenter, is a lame man of about fifty, obstinately polite, and paternally contradictory. He has a great contempt for young men, and recalls fondly the days of Farley and Tom Dibdin. He is in misty evening dress, with a limp white cravat.

Lotus, the wardrobe-keeper, has very effeminate manners, and is a tailor to the core. He is given to talking in initials. The manager having one day sworn at him, he described the circumstance tearfully to a friend in these terms: 'Mr. J. came upstairs, called me an F., and told me to go to the D.!'

Miss Crooner, the mistress of the ladies' wardrobe, is an elderly female, with grizzled hair and a curiously lean neck. Constant contemplation of brilliant hues in various fabrics, of lace and foil-paper, gold and silver, has taken every vestige of colour from her face and garments. Her manners are perfectly ladylike, and she is troubled with a short cough, as if she had swallowed a spangle and it had stuck in her throat.

Slocum, the property-maker, is a short man, whose features are deeply indented with that scourge of beauty the smallpox. He is a most ingenious fellow, and incorrigibly lazy. With every suggestion made he acquiesces fervidly, and would say, 'Yes, sir,' if it were proposed to him to jump off Waterloo Bridge. He is always behind-hand in whatever he undertakes, and has as many ingenious reasons for delay as a Foreign Secretary.

'Well,' says Mr. Hammer, when the author has read the scenes and business of the opening, ' you hear what it's all about, and I'm sure we shall all do our best. We'd a great go last Christmas, and we must try to

keep up our reputation.   You understand all about that
effect for the ghost scene, Mr. Size?'

' W-e-ll, yes—a—a—I think so,' answers that gentleman.   ' The heads to nod are Slocum's affair, of
course.'

' Yes, sir, all right, sir, I understand, sir,' says the
acquiescent Slocum.

' About my mask?' interrupts Mr. Writhe; ' you
know what I mean—about the eyes and the mouth?'·

' Yes, sir,' says Slocum.

' The springs at the jaws, so that I can work 'em?'
continues Writhe.

' All right, sir.'

' And the wig, you know?'

' Yes, sir.'

' The hair to stand bolt upright when I see the key?'

' All right, sir.'

' I—don't—see—my way clear—about—the trans-
parency—behind—the—sink and fly—and medium,'
says Boggles, slowly.   ' How is that all to be struck—
for the fairy scene—the second scene?'

Boggles always makes objections, and always has his
work done to the minute he has promised it.

' Oh—a—easy enough,' remarks Mr. Size; ' have a
double sink and fly: second and third.'

' Yes, a double sink and fly, of course!' says Mr.
Hammer.   ' Gamut (the leader of the orchestra) couldn't
come to-day.   He's up to his eyes scoring for the
drama.'

' What do you think of that notion of mine of a
comic elephant?'

' Comic elephant—yes, sir,' says Slocum.

' Well, don't see much fun in an elephant; he's so black—nothing to be got out of him. What do you think, Mr. Size ?'

' I—a—I think it's better for the elephant to—to be —a—as like the real thing as possible.'

' Real elephant—yes, sir,' says Slocum.

' Of course—real as possible,' echoes the stage-manager. ' Pleases the children—make 'em think it's alive. No! eyes and trunk and tail to work—nothing more *I* think !'

' Eyes and trunk and tail to work—nothing more— no, sir,' remarks Slocum.

' We shall be all right in your department, Miss Crooner, I know,' says Mr. Hammer, complimentarily.

' I hope so, sir,' says the gratified Miss Crooner, with a short cough.

' You understand what Mr. Writhe means about the Bluebeard dress, Lotus ?'

' Oh, quite positif, sir,' replies Lotus; ' all right I am, I know, sir. The late Mr. Thwaites used to say of me : " L. is one of those T.'s who never makes a B." '

There was a general grin, for Lotus is the butt of the theatre.

A general conversation ensues — the staff retire variously, and the stage-manager and author discuss vexed questions over bitter beer.

In theatrical parlance, the word ' plot' means a list of articles required in a particular department. A day or two after the reading, Mr. Boggles receives the following :—

PANTOMIME.

Scenes.	Scene Plot.	Wings.	Grooves.
1	Sink and fly, backed by Transparency. Set Pieces R. and L. Small trap C. open. Flaps to work. Trap to work. Face and eyes to work.	Cavern.	2
2	Fairy Scene. Set. Fountains to work. Waves to work. Grave trap to rise. See to Sandbags.		
3	Pantomime Kitchen. Boiler C. Oven L. Apparatus R. See to Explosion.	New.	2
4	Transparent Horizon. Turkish Landscape set. Cottage R. 2 E. Well L. 3 E. Vampire Tree L. 2 E. Procession to work from L. to R., &c. Sandbags.		3 and 4

and so on. When the scenery is nearly ready he is also furnished with the plots for the flies and traps :—

PANTOMIME.

Scenes.	Flies.
1	Cavern. Lower fly. 1st Bell. Take up fly.
2	New cut Fairy.
3	Burlesque Arch.
4	New pink Sky.

&c., &c.

The flies are that portion of the theatre in which are fixed the windlasses and rollers that work clouds, arch—

ways, and the upper portion of the scenery. Of the traps, down which evil geniuses disappear, and up which good fairies emerge, it is unnecessary to make any explanation :—

PANTOMIME.

TRAPS.

Lower small C.
1st Bell.—Rise small C.
2nd Bell.—Shut up small C.
3rd Bell.—Open Grave.
4th Bell.—Rise Grave.
&c., &c.

Slocum, the indolent, is put in possession of a list which causes him the most intense annoyance, as it convinces him that he will be compelled to work :—

PANTOMIME.

PROPS. (Properties).

Scenes.	PROPS. (Properties).
1	*Trick cauldron, change to cage. Large ladle. Sixteen spectacles and sixteen sticks for Witches. Two large trumpets for Heralds. Trick tail for Imp to light. Paper for Herald. Bees for cage.*
2	*Branches. Wand. Fire.*
3	*Kitchen Scene. Dish-covers, ladles, pigs, saucepans, gridirons, frying-pans (one very large), &c., &c. ; fish, poultry, joints, hams, cabbages, turnips, carrots. Large fish-kettle. Turtle (Little Munby). Large pepper-castor, mustard-pot, and salt-cellar. Steam C. Squib L. Flour-box, candles. Maroon for explosion, and squib for turtle.*
4	*Rope and windlass for well L. 3 E. Banjo for Selim. Large lanthorn for Ibrahim. Stuffed stick. Carpet-bag for Fatima. Flower-pots. Ladder ready L. 1 E. Veil and wreath for Bridesmaids. Profile procession. Seven instruments for Band. Drum for Band. Elephant (Craddock and Duffy). Straw and flowers for Selim. Rope and stick for Guard.*

&c., &c.

The same sort of plan of operations is supplied to Miss Crooner and to Mr. Lotus :—

PANTOMIME.

LADIES.

16 *Witches. Hats Change to Fairies.*
16 *Fairies, white.*
16 *Extra, blue.*
 6 *Bridesmaids* (Toogood, Schmidt, Nobbs, E. Nobbs, Croone, and Phillips).
14 *Turkish Peasants.*
 8 *Children.*
21 *Nightgowns and nightcaps for little Bluebeards.*
20 *Nightgowns for Ghosts.*

&c., &c.

PANTOMIME.

Rusticumfusticum. Red and wings.
8 *Imps.*
Little Imp. Trick tail.
6 *Cooks.*
6 *Scullions.*
8 *Attendants.*
Selim.
Fatima (Arthur Pattison).
Ibrahim.
Sister Anne (Joe Munby).
4 *Bearers.*
8 *Brass Bands.*
6 *Guards, red.*
6 „ *green.*
6 „ *blue.*
6 „ *black.*
Change for Selim (*Rags*).
Bluebeard.

&c., &c.

THE REHEARSALS.

The rehearsals, like everything else pertaining to a pantomime, are at first divided into departments. The ballet is arranged before anything else, and the corps is called at 10 o'clock. The ladies put on their practising clothes, short skirts, old shoes, and a loose jacket, and

descend to the stage—wonderfully different in their
work-a-day costume to their brilliant appearance when
they bound before the footlights in book-muslin and
coral. Mr. Fauve, the répétiteur, is seated in the
orchestra in solitary state, and dismal and dire sounds
the scrape of one violin in that large, half dark, enormous area. M. Pointdetout, the ballet-master, is seated
in a chair on the right of the stage.

'Now then, ladies,' roars Monsieur, ' we shall begin.
Mistair Fauve, if you please.'

Mr. Fauve strikes up, and the corps de ballet dance
on from various entrances, and form arches with long
pieces of cane—the canes being substitutes for the coral
branches, which the dilatory Slocum is ordered to
make.

' Slower, Miss Gross—lum—tum—tum—tum—trum
—ta—Blanche out of tune—G-r-r-r-a ! Ah !' Monsieur
claps his hands and the music stops. The corps
remains in the exact attitude they struck at the last
bar of music.

Monsieur is in a towering passion. He rises and
exclaims—

' Ah, ladies! Is it that I have lost all my trouble this
last week ? Go back! all! and Blanche, I saw you.
It is very well. You four first, Grove, Levy, Smol-
lett and Suckthumbe—what did I teach you?' Here
Monsieur goes to the wing, and, arching his arms, bounds
on to the stage, and dances with incredible lightness
for so stout a man. ' Am I to say that once more ?
It is supposed to be fairies, it is not cows ! So !'

The ballet-master claps his hands, and the music and
the dancing recommence—are stopped again—recom-

mence again, and Monsieur, ordinarily the most courtly
of Frenchmen, conducts himself like a despot and a
tyrant until they are performed to his perfect satisfaction.

The same sort of scene is being enacted in the green-
room, where Mr. Gamut, the leader, is drumming at a
piano, surrounded by those actors and actresses who
sing in the opening, and a damp and uncomfortable-
looking chorus.

'Sing out!' says Mr. Gamut. 'Let me hear you!
Now! From "War in his eyeballs glistens!"'

The chorus sing :—

> 'War in his eyeballs glistens,
> Bow, for his will is law—
> For life or death Hang on his breath,
> For life or death Hang on his breath—'

'Sing out!' interrupts the leader, singing with them.

> 'Hail to the Great Bashaw!
> Hail to the Great Bashaw!
> Hail to the Great Bash—AW ! ! !'

'I don't hear any of the words, you know,' says Mr.
Gamut, despairingly. 'I hear the notes, but I don't
hear the words! There are plenty of copies about, but
I know nobody has looked at them. Mr. Rumball!'

'Sir?' says a thin man, with a deep bass voice, that
thrills the wires of the instrument.

'Do you know the words?'

'Yes, I do, sir.'

'Sing them as a solo, then. "Mark his approach
with thunder." Now!'

Mr. Rumball growls :—

‘ Mark his approach with thunder,
      Strike on the trembling spheres—’

and then stops.

‘ Go on,’ says Mr. Gamut.

Mr. Rumball coughs.

‘ Don't you know any more?’

After a pause, Mr. Rumball says, ‘ Well, sir, to speak
the truth, 1 do not.’

‘ I thought not!’ says the injured and sarcastic
leader. ‘ There's a copy of the words, and just be
good enough to get them into your head by next rehearsal. Now, the duett!’

While the ballet and the chorus are thus employed,
the harlequin and columbine arrange the ‘ trips ’ (the
dances which commence each comic scene and are
interrupted by the voice of the clown), and the clown,
pantaloon, sprite, harlequin, and columbine the ‘ cascades ’ (the pictures and attitudes formed in the last
scene, when harlequin stands in the centre with his
spangled legs very wide apart, the sprite stands on his
head, clown and pantaloon on each side on one leg, and
columbine, elevating herself by resting one foot on
the hands of harlequin, whose fingers are clasped
behind him, makes the apex to the pose, forming altogether a sort of pantomimic coat of arms or Christmas
escutcheon). Silent and undemonstrative at the reading
of the opening, in which they are unconcerned, clown
and pantaloon here are in their full glory. All the
male pantomimists are attired in white jackets and
trousers, and columbine is in ‘ practising’ costume.
The business and conversation run in this fashion :—

‘ Hornpipe over,’ says harlequin.

Clown immediately runs on and is felled by a blow
of harlequin's bat. Clown falls flat on his back on the
stage, and walks on his elbows to the opposite side,
while harlequin shakes his bat over him. Clown suddenly turns on his face; harlequin hits him—'bats' him
is the technical term—on the back. Clown turns
again; harlequin bats him on the chest. This business
is repeated several times. Clown rises quickly to his
feet; sprite jumps over his head; clown, indignant, turns
round and hits pantaloon, who appears just in time to
receive the blow. Harlequin gives his bat to columbine,
and is seized by clown and pantaloon, and a furious
cannonade of ' slapping ' begins.

' Now, Patchy, tip us the slap !' says clown, and harlequin slaps clown, who slaps him back again—harlequin
slaps pantaloon, who slaps harlequin back again.

' Now the double !' says the clown, and clown and
pantaloon both slap harlequin, who, by an action of
both hands, slaps them again, and they fall to the
ground. During this, the sprite is in one corner standing on his head, and doing various impossibilities with
his limbs, while columbine, bat in hand, twirls, pirouettes
and poses in the other.

About a week before Boxing-night, Mr. Size having
worked indefatigably; Mr. Boggles having made every
difficulty and finally triumphed over it; Miss Crooner
having done marvels in the equipment of fairydom
and houridom; Mr. Lotus having yielded to frequent
bursts of tears, and declared that ' them actors and
actresses is the cuss o' the profession !' and Mr. Slocum
having procrastinated until he was compelled to sit up to
work all night—a fact upon which he dilated with an

air of injury—the 'call' for a full rehearsal is put up in
the hall :—

THEATRE ROYAL ————.

Monday, Dec. 20.

Ballet at 10.   Mr. FAUVE.

Pantomime at 11.   Mr. GAMUT.
                                      PROPS.
        Everybody.   SUPERS.

As a description of the rehearsal of an entire pantomime would fill a large volume, we propose to give
only a portion of a scene of the opening and of the
comic business, as there is an infinite variety of monotony, and monotony of variety, in all things belong-
ing to theatrical rehearsals.

If our readers will turn to the scene plot, it will be
found that the fourth scene of the pantomime is described as a Turkish village. The scene is set. There
is a cottage on one side of the stage, a well upon the
other, a distant country stretching from side to side.

'Now,' says the stage-manager.

Mr. Gamut and the orchestra play a slow strain of
music, and Selim appears on the stage, groping his way
as if in the dark. Selim is attired in a dark shooting-
coat and waistcoat and grey trousers; his face is hid in
an enormous mask, on the top of which is wound a
turban. The large, long head, with its staring eyes and
shiny brick-red complexion, upon the short body, gives
a grotesqueness to his figure, of which every one is

conscious but himself. Selim places his hand upon his heart, points to the window of the cottage, places his hand upon his heart again and shakes himself violently —this is presumed to convey to the audience that he, Selim, is deeply enamoured of the inmate of the cot. Selim then blows a kiss to the window, and with his right forefinger points to the third finger of his left hand—this is meant to signify that his intentions are honourable, and he means to marry his beloved. He then runs off the stage and immediately runs on again with a banjo, and plays a serenade—a parody on the popular nigger tune of 'I'm off to Charlestown.'

The ditty over—a grand crash is heard in the orchestra—the window of the cottage opens, and a large and hideous head enveloped in a nightcap looks out. This head is the property of Ibrahim, Fatima's father. Selim hides himself where everybody can see him, and the large mask at the window sneezes and drops the nightcap on the stage. How Fatima tries to elope with her lover, and how the elopement is frustrated by Sister Anne and Ibrahim, can be easily imagined by the patrons of theatres on Boxing-night.

Mr. Joe Munby, who plays Sister Anne, is the father of Dick Munby, who is only sixteen years old, and who plays Ibrahim. The paternal and filial relations are thus reversed—Joe the father proving a most tiresome and skittish child, and Dick the son a most inexorable and cruel parent.

The rehearsal goes on swimmingly until a march is played. Bluebeard's procession—a number of figures about a foot high—is seen to glide across the distant country.

'Stop—stop—stop!' says the stage-manager, rising from his chair. 'Boggles!'

Fifty voices repeat the name of Boggles.

'*Where* is he?' says the stage-manager. 'Where the deu—'

'Here I am, sir,' says Mr. Boggles, peeping over the minarets of a distant mosque—perspectively considered to be twenty miles off.

'That procession mustn't fly across in that way!'

'What's the mat-ter—with—it, sir?' inquires Boggles, with provoking calmness.

'Matter!' echoes the S. M., 'why there's supposed to be some ten miles of distant country from one end of that set piece to the other. You're making that elephant and the rest of the procession march at about the rate of twelve hundred miles an hour!'

'I—thought—you—wouldn't like the procession to—hang, sir,' objected Boggles.

'No; but such a rate as that is impossible,' returns Mr. Hammer. 'Over such a space, too.'

'It's the space that kills,' says Mr. Syllabus, the author; but nobody notices the observation.

'I—thought—you'd—wish me — to— make —some allowance—for—the—effect from the front, sir,' urges Boggles.

'*Some* allowance — yes — but not twelve hundred miles. What would the critics say?'

'Nothing,' mutters the author, 'in a whole column of print.'

'Try it again,' says Mr. Hammer.

'Ve-ry good, sir.'

'Now, once more,' says the stage-manager. 'Tum-

F

ti-tum-tum-tum-tum-tiddy-iddy-iddy-tiddy-tol-lol-de-day !'

The music recommences, and the procession marches across again from the left hand to the right—this time at only the rate of about two hundred miles per hour.

' Ah! that's all right,' says the stage-manager.

' *Stet processus*,' says the author.

' I beg your pardon ?' says the stage-manager, turning to him.

' Oh! nothing,' says Mr. Syllabus.

By this time the procession—very much grown since its last appearance—is crossing another set-piece from right to left.

The band plays *fortissimo*, the cymbals clash, and the real procession tramps on to the stage : a band with horns of gilded wicker-work, men with banners, slaves bearing presents like silvered petrifactions of fruit from Covent Garden Market, soldiers and cymbal-players. The chorus strike up :—

> ' Mark his approach with thunder !
> Strike on the trembling spheres !'

Mr. Hammer becomes excited, stamps his feet, and waves his right arm as if he were conducting an orchestra.

' Tum-ti-di-dum-tum-tum-tum,' sings Mr. Hammer. 'Turn your banner, sir '—this to a supernumerary—'row-dow-de-dow-dow-dow! Hold up that crescent, you IDIOT! You, sir—I said idiot, didn't I ? I meant you, of course. St-aup !' Mr. Hammer claps his hands, and the procession halts as if by magic.

' Slocum !' cries the stage-manager.

Fifty voices repeat ' Slocum !' There is a delay in

finding Slocum. At last he appears in a terrible bustle, a paste-brush in his hand. He had been asleep in a corner of the property-room.

'Where are these men's scimitars?' asks the enraged S. M., pointing to some 'supers.'

'Semmitars, sir?—yes, sir,' says Slocum. 'Be ready to-morrow, sir.'

'To-morrow!' thunders the stage-manager.

'Yes, sir. You said the men's semmitars would do by to-morrow.'

'Their masks, not their scimitars!'

'Masks was it, sir? Yes, sir, I think it was masks.'

'*You think! Shall* I have 'em to-morrow?'

'The masks, sir?'

'SCIMITARS!' roars the stage-manager.

'Oh! yes, sir.'

'Ugh! Go on, Mr. Gamut.'

The chorus begins again—

> 'Mark his approach with thunder!
> Strike on the ——'

'Stop!' shouts the stage-manager. 'Slocum!'

Fifty voices again repeat the magic name, and Slocum presents himself again, with a sheet of foil-paper in his hand.

'Where's the elephant?' roars the stage-manager, accompanying the question with a few oaths.

'Quite ready, sir.'

'Why don't it come on?'

'The fore-legs and the hind-legs is getting inside it, sir.'

'Why the devil weren't they inside it? Who are they?'

'Duffy and Craddock, sir — played the legs at the Garden, sir, thirty year ago.'

The stage-manager runs to the wing, behind which stands the head and body of a huge property elephant, constructed of wicker-work covered with canvas.

'Why are you not ready?' asks the S. M. of two dirty-looking men.

'We've got no legs, sir,' answers one of the men.

'Slocum!'

'Slocum!' echo the voices.

'Where are the legs?'

'Legs, sir?'

'I said legs, didn't I? I'll say it again. *Legs!* LEGS!! LEGS!!!' roars Mr. Hammer.

'Be ready to-morrow, sir,' says the active Slocum.

'To-morrow!' repeats Hammer, with a volley of strong language. 'Get inside; we'll try it without 'em.'

'I knows my business, sir,' says Mr. Duffy, who delineates the hind-legs. 'I seen the late Muster Grimaldi at the Wells when——'

Mr. Hammer cuts him short by wishing him and the late Mr. Grimaldi in Nova Scotia—but he doesn't say Nova Scotia. The two men crawl into the interior of the basket-animal and march on. Their heads and bodies are entirely concealed in the body of the elephant. Mr. Craddock, the fore-legs, wears corduroy trousers, turned up at the heels. Mr. Duffy's lower limbs are clothed in shepherd's plaid, and the effect of the huge elephant's body waddling on these singular supporters is so irresistibly ludicrous that the ladies of the ballet laugh.

'Silence!' thunders the stage-manager. 'Keep time —you men inside.'

'I knows my business, sir,' murmurs Mr. Duffy, from

the interior. 'I seen the late Muster Grimaldi at the Wells——'

'Hold your tongue! Work your trunk—you fore-legs—tum-ti-di-tum-tum-tum.'

The trunk moves up and down, and the elephant runs over a man bearing a banner.

'What are you about? Where are you going? shouts the stage-manager.

'Please, sir, I can't see,' says Mr. Craddock, from the chest of the sagacious beast.

'He never played his part before, sir,' interrupts Duffy. '*I* have. The late Muster Grimaldi, at the Wells, once said——'

'Hold your tongue! You talk too much. You're playing the hind-legs, not the jaws. The elephant's hind-legs don't talk.'

A roar of laughter follows the stage-manager's sally.

'Against all the laws of natural history as well as dramatic unity,' says the author.

'Really, Mr. Syllabus,' says the stage-manager, pettishly, 'I cannot conduct the rehearsal if I am to be interrupted in this way.'

'I presume I may make a remark?' objects the author, turning very red.

'I am here to direct, sir,' says the S. M.

'And I am here to see that you direct properly,' says the author.

'I am not to be dictated to by you, sir.'

'Nor I, sir, by you.'

'Very well, sir.'

'Very well, sir.'

A dead silence is observed by every one upon the

stage during the quarrel between the two potentates, and the rehearsal proceeds with the same sort of hitches, stoppages, and general entanglement.

The 'flats' run on for the comic scene represent a manufactory, a baker's shop, and a barber's shop. Harlequin and columbine waltz on and continue spinning till clown, behind the scenes, shouts out, 'A-i-e-a-e-a-ya! I'm a looking at you!' when the action takes place described in the rehearsal of the 'trips and cascades.'

'Seven and eight!' shouts the stage-manager, and two men bring on an odd-looking box, on which is painted, 'American Anticipating Machine.' Clown brings the two men to the front of the stage and says, 'How much?' at which the two men shake their heads gravely. Clown says, 'Three half-pence more,' and the two men nod their heads to signify acquiescence. Clown, having made the purchase, sends the two men off without payment, except the parting kick which they receive from pantaloon.

'Old gent!' says the clown, looking at the prompter.

'Nine!' shouts the prompter. 'Nine, Perkins!'

'Perkins!' roars the stage-manager.

A young man runs on breathless, and receives the compliments of the stage-manager, the prompter, the clown, and the pantaloon. After being raved at for a quarter of an hour, Perkins explains that he was looking for the dog.

'Dawg! ain't you got it, then?' asks the clown.

'Couldn't find it, sir.'

The euphonious name of Slocum again resounds throughout the theatre.

Mr. Slocum appears holding a book of Dutch metal (imitation gold-leaf).

'Dog, sir?' says Slocum, in answer to inquiries; 'dog has just stepped out with Mrs. Slocum.'

Mrs. Slocum, coupled with her worthy husband, is spoken of in a most unbecoming manner, and Slocum returns to his room.

'Twelve!' cries the prompter, and a man crosses to the baker's shop with a large dish and cover, which clown steals. Clown then says, 'I say, old 'un, let's garotte somebody,' and then clown and pantaloon hide behind opposite wings.

'Thirteen!' shouts the prompter.

A man with a mask and shoulders, over his own head and shoulders, staggers on, assuming that intoxication of the legs and feet peculiar to the stage. Clown immediately throws his arm round the mask in the place where the neck ought to be. Harlequin twirls on, slaps his bat upon the stage, and the head rolls from the man's shoulders. Pantaloon, who is robbing the victim, terrified at the sight of the headless man, falls on his face. Clown is transfixed with horror, and harlequin laughs with his shoulders and wags his head.

'Fourteen!' shouts the prompter.

The music becomes slow and mournful. A man, supposed to be a policeman, crosses, and clown puts the head in the stolen dish and puts the cover over it. When the policeman has stalked away, harlequin bats again, the dish-cover flies off, and the head rolls its eyes and opens its mouth menacingly at clown.

Clown cries, 'Now ready everybody for the spill and pelt!'

Clown endeavours to avoid the head, but harlequin
shakes his bat over it, and the head pursues the comic
garotter wherever he goes.   The policeman re-enters
and arrests clown.   In vain does clown protest that 'He
didn't go to do it.'   At last clown throws the head at the
officer of law, and hits a man laden with property-fish.
Music quick and animated.   A number of men and
boys come on and tumble over each other, apparently
with intense delight.   The policeman comes to grief.
Carrots, turnips, and fish fly in the air.   Suddenly there
is a cry of ' Gorilla loose !' and a man dressed as a gorilla
appears.   The combatants fly, and the scene is termi-
nated by the clown and the gorilla waltzing off grace-
fully together.

The prompter whistles.

' Wash-house scene,' says the stage-manager.   ' Ten,
eleven, and twelve !'

. A pantomime very often consists of six or seven
such scenes, each having different business and a sepa-
rate set of properties.   The reader may therefore
imagine that the rehearsal is no slight labour to those
intimately concerned.   It sometimes lasts nearly the
whole day, and during this time the actors and others
rarely find an opportunity to sit down and rest their
weary limbs or to partake of any refreshment beyond a
biscuit and a glass of beer.   The 'business,' which we
have described above, is repeated day after day for a
fortnight or three weeks before the production of the
piece; and in many instances the last rehearsal is not
brought to a close until within half an hour of the time
for opening the doors on Boxing-night.

CHAPTER VII.

A PEEP behind the scenes of a theatre, at the most
ordinary times, affords a strange and curious spectacle.
Nothing strikes the stranger so much as the quaint and
dingy look of everything around him. The boarding of
the stage, which, from the front, appears so well calculated for the delicate satin shoes of the dancer, is found,
on near inspection, to be rugged and worn, and inter-
sected on every hand by the projecting edges of traps.
Right and left, and at the back, when the stage is clear
of scenery, you see the rough, unplastered walls, blotched
with dark greasy spots, where painters and carpenters
have been accustomed to squeeze through behind close
sets and drawn-off flats. Looking up among the jointed
grooves projecting in all sorts of fantastic attitudes from
the 'flies,' you conceive the notion of being in an un-
finished house before the floors are laid, in which a
large number of the old wooden telegraphs have been
stored. The ropes and pulleys are suggestive of a ship,
and the sky borders of a dyer's loft. The Bowers of
Bliss and Palaces of Delight, which look so dazzling at
night, are incomprehensible smudges at close quarters
by day. Daylight takes all the romance out of the
theatre. When the lamps have gone out and the grey

dawn streams in through the dingy panes in the roof,
the royal palace down below becomes a barn. The sun
makes everything bright and gay—everything but the
theatre. Thalia and Melpomene hold their licence
from Diana.

A rehearsal! what a strange affair is that! Here
the envious daylight takes the romance, too, out of the
actors. Your Divinity of the footlights comes in draggled
from a long walk in the rain, and gets 'blown up' by
the uncouth stage-manager—stage-managers are always
uncouth, on principle—for being late. 'Now then, Miss
Divinity, how much longer are we to be kept waiting
for you?' Miss Divinity is carefully putting by her
dripping umbrella and muddy goloshes in the prompter's
box. Your comic favourite comes on with a comforter
and a cough, grumbling at his part, for which he shows
his contempt by blundering at every second word, and
going up to the author and asking what it means. The
piece is intended to be a comic one — 'a regular
screamer.' It sounds, as the words are mumbled over,
as serious as a sermon. The comic man looks as gloomy
as a vampire. The draggled divinity wears an aspect
positively repulsive. The first old man is the embodi-
ment of injury and insult combined. The second
chambermaid is a walking effigy of disgust. The first
young man, contemplating 'half a length,' is satisfied
that a piece in which he has so little to say must prove
a dead failure; the author begins to think so too. He
thought his piece funny once; but not now. Daylight
and rehearsal have taken all the fun out of it, and it
will not be restored until Miss Divinity has put on her
pretty dress, and the comic man has reddened his nose,

and the lamps are lit. A stage rehearsal is at all times
a sternly practical and business-like proceeding; and
most particularly and peculiarly so when the business in
hand is the harlequinade—the *comic scenes*, as they are
called—of a pantomime.

The young people, ay, and the old people no less,
who sit in the boxes and roar until the tears run down
their cheeks at the frolicsome waggeries of the clown,
and the amusing discomfiture which he visits upon
pantaloon and the other destined martyrs of the drama,
are little accustomed to reflect that all this extravagant
nonsense has first of all to do with tears, not of laughter,
but of pain and grief, and wearing toil. All this kicking, and slapping, and burning with imaginary red-hot
pokers, has been a very serious and painful business for
a fortnight or more before the opening night. The
clown looks a merry wag, does he not? A fellow of
infinite jest—always ready for a mad prank. You
should see him in his canvas trousers and slippers at
rehearsal, practising the slap with pantaloon, or trying
his back for a summersault. It is a long time since he
has turned head over heels, and he is not without fears
for his neck or some of his bones. Pantaloon and
harlequin are as nervous as he is, and the pyramid at
the end of the 'rally' is a failure. They have not yet
warmed to their work. They try and try again, and
fail and fail again. Roused at length by the reproach-
ful looks, if not words of the manager, they rush at it
desperately—neck or nothing—and at last the danger-
ous feat is accomplished. What follows is easy after
this point; since now the pantomimists have thrown all
care for their bones behind them. Seeing that a clown

nightly runs the risk of maiming himself for life, it is somewhat astonishing that the character should be so much coveted. The market, however, is always overstocked with clowns, and the overflow runs to pantaloons. Don't imagine, for a moment, that the pantaloon is always, or even occasionally, the old man he looks. He is generally a very young man, not unfrequently a mere youth of eighteen or twenty. He does not choose to be pantaloon, you may be sure of that. Does the aspirant after histrionic honours take to the profession that he may play Rosencrantz and Guildenstern? No; Hamlet is his mark. But as we cannot all be Hamlets, some of us must play Rosencrantz and Guildenstern. So with pantomimists. They cannot all be clowns. Some one must be pantaloon and have his fingers pinched. But these *dii minores* will have their consolation some day. When Rosencrantz goes into the country he will be nothing short of Prince of Denmark, and Pantaloon— why, he will be clown.

CLOWN.

Pantomimists appear under so many different aspects that it is not easy to fix their identity and determine their normal condition. What clowns and pantaloons do in the summer is, we believe, a mystery as profound as the authorship of Junius. All that is known about them is that they come out of their holes in a very dingy and dilapidated condition about the beginning of December, and, reversing the order of all floral things, burst into full bloom amid the frost and snow of January. A clown is a sort of human crocus, and his full bloom takes the magnificent form of a light-coloured, fluffy greatcoat, combined with a glossy hat with a broadly-braided and turned-in brim, a splendid waistcoat, and studs, rings, and chains designed and executed on the largest scale known to the jeweller's art. His diamonds, if valued according to their size, should be worth a king's ransom. It is the idiosyncrasy of the clown in private life always to make up for the heavy swell. Perhaps this may be only the natural rebound from the fool's dress, and the bumpkin's grin, and the knock-kneed walk of his footlight existence. View him in the street in all his glory. Does he look like a personage who could condescend to squash a baby or pocket a string of sausages? Can you imagine that magnificent personage turning heels over head? Can you conceive a grand seigneur like this being troubled in his mind by the loss of a fourpenny bit? Can you imagine him stretching his mouth from ear to ear, and asking you 'how's your mother?" If he were to sing, would you expect 'Tippetywitchet' or 'Hot Codlings' from him? No: *Piff-paff*, or *Suoni la Tromba*. Nor does the clown forget his dignity even when he wears the paint. Though the fluffy greatcoat, and the braided hat, and the Brobdignagian jewellery are stowed away in the dressing-room, the self-importance is all here, asserting itself royally through the thick coat of bismuth, the moment he makes his exit and reaches the wing. See him come off from bonneting a policeman, stealing a leg of mutton, or tripping-up a baker. He is no longer clown, but *Mr.* Grimaldi Jones; and the subordinates at the wing say, ' Sir,' to him; and his dresser obsequiously asks him if he would *please* to change; and to

all these respectful addresses he replies in the lofty
style of a Don Magnifico. No eminent tragedian is
more exacting of respect than the favourite clown.
And sometimes in these days he gets as high pay as the
eminent tragedian. Pretty actresses, we know, are apt
to crush the hearts of young gallants in the stalls. But
did it ever enter any one's mind to conceive that a
knock-kneed, wide-mouthed clown was, in any point of
view, adapted to crush the hearts of ladies in the boxes?
We should say, never. But still it is a fact, that clown
graces have an attraction for the fair sex. We once
knew a clown who was taken a fancy to by a lady—a
real lady, of property, too. She married him, and next
Boxing-night the clown came to the theatre in his own
carriage. He had now money enough for his support
without acting; but his wife liked to see him play
clown, and it was part of the matrimonial compact that
he should continue his profession.

PANTALOON.

Pantaloons, when they have given up all hope of
becoming clowns, and have settled down into the lean
and slippered existence, exhibit an idiosyncrasy of an
opposite kind. They do not aspire to be swells. On
the contrary, they affect extreme plainness of dress, and
sometimes even seediness. This latter, however, may
not always be an affectation. The pantaloon carries
into private life the passive characteristics which dis-
tinguish him on the stage. His demeanour, both in the
street and in society, is that of one who feels conscious
that his destiny is to suffer discomfiture and be put

upon. He appears prepared on all occasions to take and give the slap, and to suffer any accident that may happen to him with an equal mind. The force of habit remains strong within him long after he has retired from the boards. It was once our high privilege to be on intimate terms with a pantaloon—one of the old school. On a certain occasion when we took tea with him, a clothes-horse fell against him as he was in the act of buttering his muffin. In an instant he dropped the knife, gave the slap, and shied his muffin across the table at his son and heir (aged twelve), who, receiving it in the eye, returned the slap with a promptitude which clearly showed the direction of his ambition. We shall never forget the meeting which took place between our pantaloon and a retired clown of his former acquaintance. The clown had become a master chimney-sweep, and had grown stout, and wore broad-cloth. Pantaloon (also in his Sunday clothes), viewing him from the door of a hostelry, cried out in a joyful voice, 'What, Joey, is that you?' 'What, Alf!' cried the former clown—rushing to embrace his old *collaborateur*—'Tip us the slap, old boy.' And then and there on the muddy pavement, and in their suits of broad cloth, the habit of old days came back upon them, and they flapped and slapped and turned head over heels, and then grasped each other by the hand with a warmth of friendliness that was quite refreshing to witness.

Alf Jones, the pantaloon, was as much pantaloon in private life as he was on the boards. We remember a bit of domestic pantomime in which he was the chief actor which beats all the Christmas 'comic business' we ever saw. Alf was in the habit, after the performance at the theatre, of going to a shop in the neighbourhood to buy a bit of something to take home with him for supper. His wife usually went to bed, but always left a fire in the grate for her husband to cook by. One night Alf was attracted by a variety of nice-looking meats in the shop-window of a French cook near Leicester Square. There were all kinds of brawn, and rolled turkey, and potted head, and so forth; but what took Alf's fancy most was a slab of succulent-looking meat covered with rich brown jelly. Alf did not know the name of it, but he went into the shop, and pointing to the tempting brown slab with his forefinger, said :—

'I'll take half a pound of that.'

The man weighed half a pound, and wrapped it up in paper, and Alf had to pay a shilling for it.

'It's dear,' thought Alf; 'but it's tasty-looking stuff, and I'll have a treat for once.'

So Alf went home rejoicing, and found, as usual, the Missus gone to bed; but a little bit of fire was left for him in the grate. He took down the gridiron, wiped away the flavour of the morning's herring with a page of the 'Family Herald,' and put on his meat to cook.

'Now,' said Alf, 'I'll go and fetch my beer while it's doing.' So he took down the jug, whipped to the corner for the beer, and was back in a twinkling.

'Halloa!' cried Alf, as he rushed to the fire to turn his meat, 'What's up now? Gone, by Jove!'

Gone it was, clean gone, and not a vestige remained.

'It's the Missus,' said Alf. He opened the bedroom door and peeped in, but the Missus was fast asleep. 'It's the cat,' said Alf; 'I know it's the cat.' And with that he began to rout under the tables and chairs with the hearth-broom, and at length unearthing poor puss, banged her with the broom all round the room until she had scarcely one of her nine lives left in her. Having thus avenged himself, Alf drank his beer and went to bed without his supper.

Next night, on coming home from the theatre, Alf said to himself, 'I shan't be disappointed to-night; I'll get some more of that stuff, and I'll take precious good care the cat don't get it this time.' So he went into the shop, and pointing with his forefinger to a fresh slab of the brown meat, said :—

'I'll take another half-pound of that.'

He had another half-pound accordingly, and went home, and as usual found the Missus in bed asleep, and a bit of fire burning in the front room. Alf routed about for the cat, and having found her and locked her up in the coal-cupboard, put his meat on the gridiron over the fire, and went out for his beer in security. But, lo and behold! on his return the meat was gone again!

'It's the Missus,' said Alf, emphatically ; 'now I know it; now I'm sure of it.' And with that he pulled open the door and rushed into the bedroom. The partner of his bosom was fast asleep and snoring, or apparently so. 'It won't do, missus,' said Alf; 'this is the second time you've done it. Oh! it's no use your pretending to be asleep. You ought to be ashamed of yourself, you ought; as if I hadn't enough of such pantomime tricks at the theatre, without coming home to be made a pantaloon of. Give me up my meat, ma'am!' And with that Alf seized the partner of his joys by the frill of her nightgown, and shook her.

'Thieves! murder!' cried Mrs. Alf, waking up in alarm.   G

'Hush! hold your tongue,' said Alf; 'you'll wake the house.'

'What are you up to?' says the Missus, seeing who it was.

'What are *you* up to?' says Alf; 'where's my piece of meat?'

'Alf,' says the Missus, 'you're going off your nut.'

'No I aint,' says Alf; 'where's my meat?'

'What do I know about it?' she says.

'Do you mean to say you haven't took it?' said Alf.

'Took it?' she says; 'no!'

'Say, S'help your bob! you haven't.'

'S'help my bob! Alf—there!'

'Well, I'm bothered,' says Alf, 'if this doesn't beat cock-fighting! The house is enchanted, that's my belief.' And once more Alf had to go to bed without his supper.

Next night he determined that he should bring in his beer first and then put the meat down to cook, and sit and watch it until it was done. So he called again at the cook-shop, and asked for another 'half-pound of that.'

'You see,' said Alf, 'I had an accident with it last night, and the night before too. Can't think who did it; but when I had put it on the gridiron and turned my back—'

'Gridiron!' said the man.

'Gridiron,' repeated Alf.

'Ha! ha! ha!' laughed the man; 'put it on the gridiron! ha! ha! ha!'

'What are you laughing at?' asked Alf.

'Why,' said the man, 'it was—it was—ha! ha!'

'What?' demanded Alf, angrily.

'Soup,' said the man; 'mock turtle; ha! ha! ha!'

. Of course the mock turtle had run through the bars
of the gridiron almost the moment it was put on the
fire.

HARLEQUIN.

Harlequin in these days is little more than a graceful
dancer. He is generally, indeed, a teacher of dancing;
though not unfrequently, in the country, the harlequin
for the Christmas pantomime is a volunteer from the
ordinary company—some lithe and agile second walking
gentleman who is willing to don the spangles and risk
the dangers of trap leaps for a temporary addition to
his salary. The great Edmund Kean once played harlequin; and there is more than one legitimate actor of
the high-art school still living who is not ashamed to
own that he ' once upon a time ' figured as 'Patchy.'

And this reminds us what a curious and elaborate
thing a harlequin's dress is. It must be a very important article, too, in more senses than one. Its materials
are brought from all quarters of the globe, and its
manufacture, from first to last, employs a large number
of hands. Persons who are in the habit of promenading
in Bow Street cannot have failed to notice the shop of
Mr. S. May, the theatrical costumier. When all the
town is sweltering under the hot sun of June, Mr. May's
cutter may be seen (close to the door, for the conve-
nience of fresh air) mathematically chalking out the
particoloured diamonds for harlequin's Christmas attire.
He must begin at Midsummer, for the making of harlequin's dress is by no means a simple or easy matter, and
Mr. May· has thirty or forty of them to get ready by
Boxing-night. What a time of it he has, after October

commences, with clowns and pantaloons and harlequins looking in at all hours of the day to see how their finery is going on! Very earnest and anxious are the faces of these 'mad wags' on such occasions, and by no means suggestive of the genial fun which is to warm our hearts and brighten our eyes when the flowers have faded, and the leaves have fallen from the trees, and the sun has grown distant and pale and cold, like a friend who has become rich and moved into another sphere. All through June, July, and August—indeed, up to within a week of Boxing-night, you may see Mr. May's cutter slashing into great breadths of coloured Leicester and Bradford cloths, manufactured expressly for the jacket and 'pants' of harlequin. The foundation, or ground-work, of harlequin's dress is cut from the finest white cloth, manufactured exclusively at Leicester. The ground-work used to be white silk, but this white cloth is better, because it is as elastic as the material of a stocking. The coloured diamonds are cut from the finest cloths of Bradford, and are sewn together with great nicety, and in regular progression. There are, altogether, 308 pieces in a harlequin's dress. After this comes the process of spangling.

But, first, what is a spangle? Viewing them from a distance, spangles have the appearance of the sheen of silver tissue; but they are not part and parcel of the cloth. Each spangle is an individual, and has to be sewn on by itself, as a shirt button is sewn on—indeed, a spangle has exactly the shape of a shirt-button. It is a little round flat piece of glittering metal, with a hole through its centre. The process of manufacture—a monopoly of the Germans—is curious. Spangles are made of fine copper-wire,

plated with silver. The wire is drawn to the required
fineness, then turned on a slender mandril, then twisted
into the form of a brace spring or curl, then cut into
lengths. These lengths of curled wire being dropped
on a flat surface assume the shape of rings, as the
reader can readily imagine, and a hydraulic press or
hammer coming down on them, squeezes them into
solid flat discs. On a harlequin's dress there are no less
than 48,000 of these spangles, and each one of these is
picked up and sewn on separately by women. The
weight of the spangles on a dress is about three pounds,
and it takes 144,000 stitches to sew them on; that is to
say, three stitches to each spangle. During November
and December Mr. May has from twenty to thirty
people, chiefly women, employed exclusively upon
dresses for the pantomimes. Mr. Clarkson, of Wel-
lington Street, is fully employed, during the same time,
in the manufacture of pantomimic wigs; and other
tradesmen are occupied with stockings, and shoes, and
jewels, and masks, and cutlery, all devised expressly for
stage use.

COLUMBINE.

Some dancers are born columbines, some achieve that
position, and some have it thrust upon them. When
clown, or harlequin, or pantaloon, or columbine has a
daughter, and she has a good face and figure, she may
be said to be born a columbine. Familiar to her sight
from infancy are the spots, bosses, and enormous
pockets of 'Vampo,' the spangled, coloured triangles
of 'Patchy,' and the pyramidal wig and beard of the
'old 'un.' She practises *battéments* as soon as she can
toddle, and stands with her little nose close to the wall,

not as a punishment, but in order ' to turn her out '—
that is, both her feet are placed against the wall, and
she must keep them level with it. From this early
preparation, and her pantomimic parentage, she becomes columbine, and we hope, as the story-books say,
' lives happy ever after.'

The few columbines who have their pantomimic
queendom thrust upon them are generally girls whose
parents are comfortably situated as to means, and who
have no personal ambition. ' Ah !' said Monsieur
Pointdetout, the ballet-master, to us, speaking of a
columbine of this class, ' what a be-yeautiful dan-seur
that Annie Joyce would be, if she had but brains ! but,
helas ! she wants them there,' tapping his forehead.
' She is hand-some—she is gracious—she dance well—
she has a beautiful point—but brains—bah ! va !'

Last Christmas a large number of children were
engaged for a scene in which they had to build a fairy
house with the usual fairy Genius-of-the-Lamp ra-
pidity. One little girl, thoroughly *au fait* to the business, appeared tearful and discontented. She was
about eight years of age. At last she threw down her
property trowel, and advancing to the author of the
opening, said, 'Mr. B—, I address you as the author of
the pantomime. I was engaged here last Christmas,
and the Christmas before, and I gave every satisfaction.
I was in the morris-dance that used to be encored.
Last year I was in the front row ' (here the tears began
to rise), 'and this year Mr. Locksley (the stage-
manager) has put me in the back. Boo-hoo !' By the
author's intercession the child was reinstated in the
front rank. When we heard the anecdote, we said to
ourselves, ' That girl will be a columbine !'

CHAPTER VIII.

CONCLUSION.

IT perhaps never occurred to you, Materfamilias, sitting smiling in the dress circle, with your olive branches around you, that columbine, who is frisking and pirouetting before you, is herself a materfamilias, and that while she is tripping about here in short gauze petticoats, she has little ones of her own tossing about in their beds in some cheerless lodging, anxiously waiting for mother's step on the stairs. She and harlequin play the lovers well, do they not? They are all youth and grace, and smiles and airiness. Yes; and they have been man and wife these dozen years, and have had their cares and their joys, their gladness and their sorrow, like the real people who sit around you. It is well to look at them as real people. We can the better appreciate the praiseworthy efforts which they make—in the only way they can—to do their duty. And what a strange sphere it is from our point of view! The eldest of harlequin and columbine—a youth of fourteen—is now standing at the wing—he is call-boy—witnessing his father and his mother dancing. Fancy yourself, Materfamilias, with Paterfamilias in those clothes, you in the short gauze petticoats, and he in the spangles, doing a cracovienne in the presence of your son! Thank your stars that you have better work to do; but it is not harder nor sterner work than this.

The individualities of pantomimists are exhibited in a
striking light at a morning rehearsal, when the un-
romantic daylight streams down upon them. One
thing perplexes you very much, and that is, among
the motley crowd at the wing to determine who is who.
Two men in canvas trousers with white skull-caps on
their heads are busying themselves in front. Who are
they? Clown and pantaloon. But which is which?
It would be difficult to guess from their present appearance, for they have left off the clothes of the outer
world, and have not yet endued themselves in the distin-
guishing garments of the pantomine. And this crowd
of men, women, and children of all ages, sizes, and
apparent conditions—who are they? Some of the men
are of clerical aspect and wear black, somewhat rusty,
and shiny hats of the respectable chimney-pot order.
A good many of them are grizzled with age, and bear
the stamp of care upon their brows. The women are a
thin, poorly-clad, anxious-looking set; most of them
with children in their charge—some of them little mites
of things, not more than three or four years old.
There is an air of combined poverty and respectability
about this motley crowd which sadly puzzles the
stranger. He would scarcely guess that they are there
to represent shopkeepers, and policemen, and butchers,
and bakers, and the other personages of the pantomime,
whom it is the business of the clown to buffet and ill
use. They have had an anxious time of it for a week
past for fear they should not be engaged. You may
have seen them in a crowd, waiting round the stage
door in the cold, day after day. So anxious have they
been for an engagement at a shilling a night, or per-

haps less, to be tripped up, and bonneted, and burned
with pokers, and banged with shutters! The moment
it got wind that there was a frog scene in the piece,
the manager was inundated with offers of children.
The mothers of the neighbourhood went from one to
another, and spread the report of frogs, and the would-
be representatives of frogs came upon the manager like
a plague of Egypt. And when, at length, the order
went forth, ' no more frogs,' there was wailing and
lamentation outside the stage door in the cold. It is
curious, almost pitiful, to see little children, who can
barely speak, sent on to the stage to amuse others—
they who have never had a toy to amuse themselves.
We have seen little human frogs and human rats
hushed to sleep in the corner of a dressing-room until it
was time to put them into their pasteboard skins.

Fancy that, Materfamilias—a babe just weaned earning its mother's Sunday dinner! We know two little,
chubby, black-eyed things, a boy and a girl, whose heads
scarcely reach above our knee, who have been earning the
Sunday dinner of a whole family for three months past.
The independence of their behaviour in the theatre,
owing to their childish unconsciousness of any authority,
forms a striking contrast to the obsequiousness of the
grown-up employés. One day we saw the manager
passing through behind the scenes, and carpenters and
scene-shifters made way for him, and high-placed
officials and leading gentlemen and ladies bowed and
kotowed with respectful awe. So far the progress of the
manager was that of a terrible potentate through the
ranks of his subjects. But presently the great man
entered the green-room, and there our two little

chubby, black-eyed friends were engaged in boisterous
play, jumping on and off the sofas and chairs. Did
they stop their play and sneak away into a corner with
scared looks? Not they. They continued their
romping and jumping quite unconcerned; and when
the manager told them in awful tones to be quiet, the
little black-eyed boy said 'Shan't!' and the little black-
eyed girl ran against the great man, and slapping him
in a child's wayward manner, plainly told him this bit
of her little innocent mind—'I don't like you!' Bless
their little hearts, they had no idea of a great Bashaw
of a manager who held engagements in his hands and
paid salaries on Saturday. They only knew that
mother brought them there, that they played little
frogs, and that somehow or other—through mother—
money came of it, and a nice baked dinner on Sunday.

It is proverbial that one half the world does not
know how the other half lives. The rehearsal of a
pantomime sometimes helps One-half-the-world's ignorance. Among that motley, mouldy throng of supernumeraries waiting at the wing there are men who
have been educated and brought up as gentlemen;
there are decayed tradesmen; there are clerks and
shopmen out of employment; there are poor artisans of
the superior class; there are faded coryphées who once
upon a time were pets of the ballet and the admired
divinities of the stalls. Most of them have had a
theatrical connection all their lives. The decayed
tradesman has served the theatre perhaps; or he has
had customers among actors. The clerk may have
dabbled in theatrical copying. These are all thoroughly
up in their business, and take their kicks and slaps and

trippings-up with methodical and unruffled precision. For a new comer, however, the ordeal is a painful one, and if he be a superior person, it is rarely that he passes through it with success; neither his will nor his poverty will make him consent to shake his leg when a red-hot poker is put in his pocket. A case in point rises in our memory. The usual front scene of shops was set, and a pale, anxious-looking young man, who stood in the front of the crowd at the wing, was ordered by the clown to 'go on.' The young man advanced nervously and the clown followed and put the painted poker in his pocket. The youth walked on placidly and made his exit, at the opposite side, as if nothing had happened. Of course the clown was disgusted. 'That will never do; come back.' The young man came back, rather sulkily, and went through the business again, but without expressing the desired amount of comic pain—indeed, without expressing any at all. The clown was now losing his temper, and he roared out—'Now, would you walk off as quietly as that if you had a red-hot poker in your pocket? That's a red-hot poker, young man; look at me.' Here the pantaloon practised on the clown, and the clown went into the most exquisite contortions. 'Now then, try again;' and the clown roughly took the young man by the collar to bring him back to his place; but he had scarcely touched him before the young man, whose face was scarlet with indignation, first 'squared up' at clown, and then bursting away from him, rushed precipitately off the stage and out of the theatre. 'Ah!' said clown, 'he's too much of a gentleman for the work.' Which was just the truth.

A prime minister during the time of a great international difficulty is the popular *beau idéal* of a harassed man ; but we question if any prime minister, at such a time, ever worked harder, or suffered more anxiety, than does the property-man, or the stage-manager of a theatre during the production of a pantomime. For the information of such as are not versed in theatrical affairs, we may explain that ' properties' is the name given to all the articles used in the business of a scene. Tables, chairs, bedsteads, trick-boxes, carrots, snowballs, fairy wands, seaweed, locomotive engines, tobacco pipes, babies, thunder and lightning, and a thousand other things too numerous to mention, are included under the denomination. All these things have to be made and got ready, sometimes on the shortest notice. It is rarely, indeed, that they are all finished until some days after the opening night. We once heard an author complimenting a property-man for having done his work so well and in so short a time. ' You must have had hard work over it.' ' Hard work ! Why, sir, I call this nothing; when I was getting up the pantomime at the —— Theatre I never had my clothes off for four days and nights before it was produced, nor for four days and nights after it was produced—except to play harlequin.' That was his only refreshment. Nor does the property-man's anxiety cease when the work of manufacture is over. Every night, when we are shaking our sides at the mad pranks which the clown plays with his canvas turnips and calico sausages, he is toiling and sweating behind, getting all these things ready. Each scene requires its own particular set of properties, and when one set is taken away

another must immediately be brought in to supply its
place. The red herrings and the ducks, and the quartern loaves which fly about so miscellaneously in front,
must all be in their proper places at the wing. Then
there are innumerable trick-boxes to drag out and
prepare; one little boy has to be put into one, and
another little boy into another, and great care must be
taken that all the strings and flaps are in proper working order. A vast amount of strong language is required to help these multifarious arrangements to their
due consummation. A stage-manager will tell you
that it is as impossible to do without strong language
during the performance of a pantomime, as it is to
command a man-of-war without it, in a gale of wind.
Speak 'genteelly' to your scene-shifter or your fore-
mast-man, and a trap sticks, or away go your topsails.
But the stage-manager and the prompter have plenty of
work of their own to do besides the ' ungenteel' urging
of others. Look at that elaborate business plot which
the prompter has spread out before him in his box.
Every leap, every flap change, every trap trick is there
marked down; and the prompter must be ready on the
instant to give the signal to those working them behind
the flats, on the flies above, and in the galleries under
the stage. A second too late with a signal and the
trick is spoiled, or, worse still, some one is hurt by
being shot against a shored trap or a buttoned door.
The dangers to which pantomimists are exposed are
more serious and more constantly imminent than the
public have any idea of. Supposing, when the harlequin leaps through the trap in the flat, that the four
men appointed to catch him are not at their posts.

Why, poor harlequin comes down with a crash on the hard boards, and perhaps maims himself for life. It is one of the great grievances of pantomimists that they cannot get these men to attend to their duties, unless by constantly feeing them, or treating them to beer. There have been many instances where these men have absented themselves on purpose to ' serve out ' a clown or pantaloon who has refused or neglected to comply with their exactions. It is a pity that the law does not provide a special punishment—and it could not be too severe—for such criminal neglect and wilful malice.

Having attempted to give some idea of the vast resources which are called into play, of the anxious and heavy labour which is gone through, and of the serious dangers which are encountered, during the performance of a pantomime, it only remains for us to speak of the great mystery which is involved in the concoction and designing of the so-called comic business. We know all about the opening. We are informed a month beforehand that such and such a popular author will write the introduction, and in due time it is presented to us—in return for sixpence—in the form of a book, with the author's name and a record of his dramatic triumphs on the title-page. But who is the author of the comic business?—the opening is not regarded as comic—who arranges those sometimes smart hits at the passing events of the day which are pantomimically carried out by clown and pantaloon? From what fertile and facetious brain proceeds the notion of turning a sack of alum into quartern loaves, Mr. Spurgeon into a gorilla, and transforming the label on a box of American pills, into ' National Debt 1,000,000,000

dollars?' Does any one imagine that these are im-
promptu funnyments, or that their design is left to
clown and pantaloon? Perhaps the matter never occu-
pies a thought. Be it known, however, that there are
authors of the harlequinade, as well as of the burlesque
opening, and that all the business is written down on
paper with equal minuteness and care, though the production is never printed in a book, and the name of the
author is never glorified in the newspapers. Let us
break through the envious silence which has hitherto
been preserved with regard to such important matters
and present our readers with a copy of a portion of the
MS. of a comic scene, as it is written down for the
pantomimists :—

'Enter clown and pant. Man × with boards, (× be it understood, means "crosses"), written on, "Just arrived, the New American
Anticipating Machine." C. purchases it, and they place it against
door of warehouse and exit' (sic). 'An old gentleman enters with
little dog. Pant. gives him bill. Clown steals dog. Old gent.
exits. Clown pops dog into machine, turns handle, and pulls out
from other side long row of sausages. Gent. returns, calls and
whistles for dog. The sausages commence wagging, á la dog's tail.
Gent. frightened, and runs off. Baker's man places board at door,
"Bakings carefully done." A boy brings on dish and cover. Clown
says, "All right," and places it on c. of stage. Calls pant. He
takes off cover, and discovers a sheep's head and potatoes. He is
about to steal one when the sheep's eyes become illuminated and
work. C., frightened, pops on cover and runs off.'

———

'Clown enters with a shabby hat, old coat, and bludgeon (à la
burglar) from chemist's shop. A gent. comes out of door. Clown
walks behind him, steals book from pocket—at same time policeman
enters—secures him. Clown begs for mercy—takes out a scroll,
written on, "*I'm a victim to kleptomania.*" Policeman holds up
another scroll—"*I'm the cure for that.*" Har. waves : Clown's scroll
changes to "*Twelve months' hard labour.*"'

And now we will conclude with the statement of a fact which we suspect is ' not generally known,' viz., that the pantomime which finds so many people in bread at Christmas-time is in many instances the sole sustaining prop of the house. At some theatres there is no profit made except at pantomime-time. All the rest of the year it is hard struggle to make both ends meet until Boxing-night comes again. And when the curtain falls for the last time on the concluding glories of the pantomime of this Christmas, the manager will send for the property-man and the scene-painter, and will instruct them to begin without a day's delay to prepare for the next, which will be performed for the first time on the 26th of December, 1863.

FINIS.

LONDON: PRINTED BY W. CLOWES AND SONS, STAMFORD STREET AND CHARING CROSS.

3802 X

CPSIA information can be obtained at www.ICGtesting.com
Printed in the USA
LVOW070149281112

309059LV00022B/1700/P